PSYCHEDELIC INTEGRATION 101

Psychedelic Integration 101

Creating Lasting Change Through Visionary Experiences

JOSEPH WALTERS

The Positive Veteran

CONTENTS

~ 1 ~
Forward
1

~ 2 ~
History
6

~ 3 ~
Mechanism of Action
14

Part 1: Pre-Ceremony

~ 4 ~
Awareness
18

~ 5 ~
Intentions
24

~ 6 ~
Practices & Routines
27

~ 7 ~
Diet
33

~ 8 ~

Reflection Questions
37

~ 9 ~

Journey Checklist
45

~ 10 ~

Red Flags
50

Part 2: During-Ceremony

~ 11 ~

Dosages
54

~ 12 ~

Set & Setting
58

~ 13 ~

Setting The Container
61

~ 14 ~

Facilitation
63

~ 15 ~

Stages of the Journey
67

~ 16 ~
Letting Go
72

~ 17 ~
Journaling & Creative Outlets
77

Part 3: Post-Ceremony

~ 18 ~
What is Integration?
82

~ 19 ~
After Care
86

~ 20 ~
Integration Pitfalls
89

~ 21 ~
6 Pillars of Integration
94

~ 22 ~
Habits & Routines
115

~ 23 ~
Self Talk
128

~ 24 ~
Final Words
133

~ 25 ~
References
136

~ 1 ~

FORWARD

Welcome to the psychedelic integration guidebook for creating lasting change through your visionary experiences. First off, I want to say thank you. Thank you for investing in yourself and for showing up to deepen your knowledge and your relationship to plant medicines.

I am going to start this book by filling you in with who I am and what brought me to bring this resource to the masses. My name is Joe Walters. I'm a psychedelic integration coach, plant medicine facilitator, holistic wellness practitioner, military veteran, and someone who has really been through the process of integration firsthand. While this book is not about me, I wanted to take some time to give you some insights into my journey and what I've been through to get to where I am today.

My journey with visionary plant medicines began after I got out of the military in 2015. At that time, I was running my own construction company that I had started with the last of my savings. Things were going great, and my company was seeing some great successes in the industry that I was in. On the outside, it appeared everything was going perfectly to plan in my life. The thing was that I was really suffering mentally, and I found myself in the depths of a deep depression. At that time, I was battling with suicidal thoughts, excessive substance abuse, severe anger issues, as well as PTSD from various unresolved past traumas of my life. Things were really reaching a boiling point within me, and I was none the wiser to it. That was the point in my life when the mushroom medicine found me.

My first experience in psychedelics consisted of me taking a dose of psilocybin mushrooms at my house with my partner, Dariana. That first mushroom experience proved to be the most pivotal experience of my life. That night, all the (false) beliefs that I had held about myself were shattered. I experienced what is commonly referred to as an ego death, or as I like to refer to it as an ego integration.

The ego serves as our sense of self. It allows us to identify as an individual and make sense of our reality. During an ego "death" experience, the part of the brain that deals with this sense of self are shut off and there is an experience of oneness with all things. This can show up in a variety of ways for different people and can be experienced with varying levels of difficulty.

For me, that is really where my true healing journey began. That experience was just the beginning. It allowed me to see a different way of being and a different way of feeling that I really didn't know was possible before. It allowed me to detach from the heavy emotions that I had identified with and understand that I'm something much more than my emotions, thoughts, and feelings. From that point on, I became obsessed with learning more about personal development, spirituality, psychology, and of course plant medicines. I read books, I listened to podcasts, I attended webinars, and I continued to journey with these healing medicines on a regular basis. It took me years to get to where I'm at today. The plant medicine experiences that I have had over the years have only ever shown me the areas within myself that I needed to heal and bring love, compassion, and understanding to. It was the work outside of the ceremonies and plant medicine use that truly led to me becoming the man I am today.

Let me tell you, it was a long road of ups and downs for me. There were a lot of beliefs, programs, ways of being, and friends that I needed to release as I made space for this new version of me to emerge. I'm certainly not perfect and I'm certainly not done healing and growing. I feel we never truly are done growing and evolving in the human experience. But I do stand here today, proud of who I am and who I have become because of the work that I put in. This is largely due to the doors that these medicines have opened within me. I'm proud to say that I'm no longer a slave to my triggered reactions. Now I can say that more times than not I am able to respond to life rather than react. Having this incredible history with the medicine and the healing that came from it, I have such a deep passion for this work that I get to do daily.

I understand that taking these medicines is just one part of the process. Integration of the medicines is a whole different aspect of it. When you put the two of them together, wow, such amazing change and transformation can come from it. That has been my journey. That's why I do what I do. And that's why I'll never stop doing this work and helping guide others through their own journey of inner healing. I also mentioned that I'm a holistic wellness practitioner. All that means is that I see the mind, body, and spirit as one cohesive unit. I don't separate these parts of our being. I think our health, our mind, our body, our emotions, all tie in together. So, when we have an emotional illness that can ultimately affect our physical health. That's what I mean by that. Looking at a person as one whole entity and not splitting them up into these different areas that don't relate to one another, as a lot of times modern western medicine does. I am also a military veteran. I was in the United States Marine Corps and served from 2011 to 2015. Before that, I was a volunteer firefighter in my town from the age of 14 until I left for the Marines at the age of 23. So, I spent most of my life fully immersed in very male-dominated cultures where competition, shit-talking, and a tough exterior shell were the name of the game to get by. All this time in these environments left me with a lot of reprogramming to be done once my journey of personal development started. This also gave me the blessing of incredible insights into the toxic male mindset that perpetuates the male population right now. I am grateful for the path I have walked as I am able to use my past to help others break free of who they are told they should be and step into who they authentically are and who they were truly meant to become on this planet. I see it as evolving beyond the toxic masculine paradigm and into the divine masculine role that will help to bring balance to this planet once again.

That was a little bit about my backstory, where I came from, and why I have such a deep passion for what I do. Now I am going to cover the flow of this book and what that looks like. This book is broken down into 3 main parts which are the pre-ceremony, during-ceremony, and post-ceremony phases. In the pre-ceremony phase, I'm going to start by going over a brief history of the three main medicines that will be discussed in this book. I am going to go over some of the mechanisms of action, which is how the medicines interact with your body physiologically. I will also be covering tips on how to best prepare yourself physically and mentally for any upcoming experiences you have planned. This section will also have insights into some red flags and cautions to look out for to ensure that you are in the right space both physically and mentally to have a psychedelic experience or if further guidance is recommended. This can literally be some truly lifesaving information. In the during-ceremony portion, I will go over what you may expect during an experience as well as tips and tricks to implement so that you can have as smooth of an experience as possible. While I can never guarantee an easy experience, there are things that you will be able to implement to ensure that you make it through to the other side with insights to take moving forward into your life. Finally, the post-ceremony portion of the book is all about the integration process. Like I mentioned, having the experience is one thing and integrating those experiences is another piece of that puzzle. I share the habits and routines that allowed me to take the lessons I learned inside of my psychedelic experiences and turn them into lifelong change. I share my 6 pillars of integration and how taking the time to look at each of those pillars is so crucial during your integration process.

So now that you know a bit more about me and what you can expect from this book it is time to get into it! Again, I want to congratulate you for taking the time to deepen your knowledge and to put the time and energy into getting the most out of your visionary experiences. With the conscious use of medicines along with the insights of this book, you are certainly on a path of massive personal development and self-growth.

~ 2 ~

HISTORY

First off, I want to talk about the three different types of psychedelics that I am going to be focusing on in this book along with a brief history of them in our culture. While there is a vast array of different psychedelic compounds that have different incredible benefits and effects, in this book I will be focusing on psilocybin mushrooms, lysergic acid diethylamide (LSD), and ayahuasca. Other commonly explored psychedelics include Peyote, Bufo, Ketamine, Kambo, Mescaline, MDMA, and plenty more that I haven't listed here. The focus of this book is on the three mentioned above as I have the most personal experience with them. Also, they are some of the most readily available as well as they are some of the most explored psychedelics from my experiences and feedback from the community.

First, we have psilocybin mushrooms also known as "magic" mushrooms. We see the uses of these plants dating back millenniums, as far back as 9,000 BC through cave paintings and ancient texts. There is a lot of evidence of this medicine being utilized in the Aztec and Mayan cultures. They have been referred to as the "flesh of the gods" which comes as a translation of the word Teonanacatl, from the Aztec culture. The Aztecs considered them to be holy sacraments and were consumed during spiritual rituals to heal the body and spirit. You can see these sacraments acknowledged in cave paintings and in the ancient texts of the time. They would also have pieces of pottery that would honor and represent this mushroom medicine. These pieces were utilized to serve the mushrooms and paid respect to this medicine that they so highly regarded. This is a medicine that's been used for thousands and thousands of years by our ancestors in ceremonial ways for different types of healing from the physical to the emotional and mental. There's a deep and rich history throughout cultures around the world on every continent of using mushrooms in various ways to assist in the collective healing process. They served as a bridge to the realm of gods and played a pivotal role in ancient societies.

Fast-forwarding a bit to the 1950s, it came to Western society. This is thanks to the then vice-president of JP Morgan at the time, a guy by the name of R. Gordon Wasson. He traveled to the Mexico mountains and partook in mushroom ceremonies with indigenous tribes down in the area. Wasson and his wife became one of the first "westerns" to partake in an indigenous medicine ceremony in the village of Huautla de Jímenez with the infamous mushroom shaman Maria Sabina. Gordon was profoundly affected by his experience, and he knew that he had to bring knowledge of this medicine to the masses in America. He proceeded to document his experience and share it with the world via magazine. He ended up publishing an article in Life magazine which was entitled "Seeking the Magic Mushroom". This is where the term "magic mushroom" got coined and popularized. He put this information out there for all to see and it began to have a ripple effect. America started to see a lot of benefits coming from this medicine finding its way into the United States. At that time, we had Albert Hoffman, Timothy Leary, Richard Albert (which many people know as Ram Das), and the McKenna brothers (Terrence and Dennis) who were deep into the studies of various visionary substances.

These were some of the leading people in the psychedelic space at that time. Leary was working for Harvard, conducting important studies into the benefits that these compounds had to offer on mental and physical health. They were seeing a lot of breakthroughs happen with these medicines in short periods of time. Unfortunately, the mushrooms became a victim of the 1970s push for the war on drugs and the big attack on the counterculture that we saw on LSD, mushrooms, and all psychedelics which were grouped together. They were labeled as bad, and the lie was perpetuated that they had no medicinal value and then they were just shoved under the rug. All further research and trials were abruptly stopped. Luckily, we're going through a psychedelic renaissance right now where we're seeing these trials start back up. Although we lost out on years of important research, we are now seeing some of the biggest universities in the world doing studies and coming back to confirm what we have confirmed before. That these plant medicines have immense healing properties in ways that we don't even fully comprehend yet.

Next, we have Lysergic Acid Diethylamide which is commonly known as LSD or "Acid". This was first synthesized in 1938 by a Swiss chemist who goes by the name of Albert Hoffman. Albert Hoffman was working for a company that was looking for a new stimulant to release at that time. During this process, he synthesized LSD 25, which the number 25 is the 25th variant of this certain chemical compound. At the time they were doing animal trials of these compounds and there did not appear to be any effect on the animals that were tested. So it went on the back burner, but Hoffman recalls that he always had this peculiar sort of feeling about this compound. He always had this internal knowing that there was something different about it. Five years later, in 1943, he went to re-examine this LSD 25 mixture. He ended up accidentally ingesting a small amount of it through his skin while doing an experiment. He perceived what he described as "extraordinary shapes with an intense kaleidoscope play of colors".

Any of you who have dabbled with LSD should be able to relate to what he's saying there and understand what he means by that statement. He was experiencing the common visual effects that LSD can unlock during its use. This piqued his interest very much. He said to himself, well that was a weird effect and there's certainly something more going on with this. So, three days later, he boldly decided to take a larger dose of this magical compound. That day was April 19th, 1943. This date is now infamously known as bicycle day. That day, Albert Hoffman took a larger dose of LSD, but he really had no frame of reference to understand what was going to happen to him. He didn't know anything about dosages or what the experience would be like. He took what would be the first intentional LSD trip and began to feel weird. Visuals that were much more intense than the day before sank in and he began to experience extreme shifts in his perception of reality. He grabbed one of his coworkers and said, "Hey, I'm feeling really weird. Can you help me get home?" Due to the vehicle shortage at the time, Albert and his co-worker were taking their bikes to work. And this is where we get to the term "bicycle day".

They decided to take a bicycle ride to get home and that is when things got intense for Albert. He said it was very difficult at various times throughout his experience. He ended up having a doctor come to his house after getting home but the doctor couldn't come close to comprehending what he was going through. Albert was certainly going through bouts of paranoia and was unsure if he had poisoned himself and was ultimately dying. The doctor checked him out and made the conclusion that physically he was alright and that this was a mental experience more than anything. As Hoffman was able to release the fear and give in to the experience, he was then able to begin to emerge on the other side with feelings of peace, gratitude, and love. I am sure that was one intense bike ride through the city, but he made it home and made it through this first LSD experience. From that point on he understood fully that there was something really going on with this formula. Just like the psilocybin mushrooms, LSD became entrenched in the 1960's counterculture and eventually came into the crosshairs of America's war on drugs.

LSD came to the United States through the CIA. You can look up an operation called MK ultra. They tried to use LSD to brainwash soldiers and manipulate them to do certain things. Anyone who's taken a psychedelic understands that they have the exact opposite effect on a person's psyche. Through these trials with the LSD, that the CIA imported, many of the people in the studies ended up taking samples out of the trials and were like "hey everyone, check this out and open your eyes". The LSD craze of the sixties really blossomed from the importing of the LSD through the CIA operation. Unfortunately, the way it went was that people were using it a bit too freely and openly. There were people advocating that everyone should be taking this substance and there was a bit of a lack of regard as to the use of this extremely powerful compound. The government stepped in with a very heavy hand. They ripped it out of the hands of all research and out of every university's hands as well. They wrongfully labeled it as having no medicinal value. Then came the 1970's and the war on drugs. LSD, just like mushrooms, became another victim of that and so did the mental health industry. We saw it just go away and underground until this recent renaissance that we're experiencing right now.

And finally, I will be discussing Ayahuasca. Commonly referred to as "Grandmother", Ayahuasca is a blend of a plant and bark that is found in the Amazon. The active component in Ayahuasca that affects you is Dimethyltryptamine or DMT. DMT is something that's naturally occurring in our bodies as well as all throughout nature. We have found it in both plants and animals. What happens with Ayahuasca is that it is a blend of a particular leaf and a particular bark that has a specific chemical makeup. If you just ingested the plant containing the DMT, your body would just synthesize it quickly and it would be flushed out of your system without having any noticeable effects on you. What happens when you have a certain chemical within you, called an MAOI, is that the DMT can stay in your system for much longer and you are able to have profound and often life-changing experiences. An MAOI is a Monoamine Oxidase Inhibitor and all that means is it doesn't allow the DMT to get broken down by a particular enzyme in your body and the effects of the DMT can last much longer.

Looking at Ayahuasca's history, we see most of the uses of this blend in South America, primarily in the Amazonian areas which include Peru, Colombia, and Ecuador. There is an ongoing debate as to how long this medicine has been utilized by ancient cultures. Many believe that there is a 5,000-year history in the Amazon cultures but there is no archaeological evidence to support this. This is in large because the people of the Amazon did not utilize written language at that time. Recently, in 2010, a pouch has been discovered with organic leftovers that match that of an ayahuasca blend. This finding had been dated to the year 1,000, so roughly 1,000 years ago. Many shamans claim that the origins of the Ayahuasca blend came from visions and dreams that pointed the shamans of the time to the specific ingredients that needed to be mixed. When Christian missionaries from Spain first encountered tribes utilizing this medicine in the 16th century they described it as "the work of the devil" and it did not begin its journey up north just quite yet. Ethnobotanist Richard Schultes dedicated his life to working with hallucinogenic plants and understanding these powerful medicines that shamanic tribes were working with down south. His book "The Plants of The Gods: Their Sacred, Healing, and Hallucinogenic Powers" (1979), along with his other published works, really opened the door for western society to explore this new experience. It became even more widely known and understood when the McKenna brothers published their ayahuasca experiences in their book "True Hallucinations" (1989).

This medicine is not limited to the Amazon areas anymore and by now it has planted its roots all over the world. People travel all over the world to work with various tribes and facilities that have shamans who act as a guide for their visionary experience. Shamans (should) have extensive experience with not only the medicine but also with being a link between the physical and non-physical planes of existence. Ayahuasca can take a person to the various depths of their psyche and have a broad range of both physical and mental effects. It is important, as with all psychedelics, to be surrounded by people who know how to support this type of experience and handle difficult situations as they may arise. Over the past few decades, we've really seen an uptake in curiosity from people around the world wanting to experience this medicine. This includes celebrity figures as well. We have the internet connecting everyone, we have social media sharing these stories and the word is out there of the profound and life-changing experiences that these medicines are offering to people. This is leading to the medicine reaching a much broader range of people and sending a lot of people traveling for this potential of healing. Also, this medicine has been making its way to the United States which has proved to be a double-edged sword. This increase in popularity has also led to its misuse and abuse both inside and outside of the states.

There have been stories coming to light of what's now being referred to as "predatory shamanism". This is where facilitators are taking people that are coming in for these very vulnerable experiences and taking advantage of that. It is something that is very unfortunate and something that we must keep a firm eye on both as a practitioner of the medicine and as someone looking to trust in someone as they go through these experiences. We must be very aware of who we're allowing to guide us through these very intense and profound experiences because we are often in very vulnerable states while taking these substances. While it's great that these medicines are reaching a lot of people and there's a lot of healing they are doing, we must be careful at what costs and how it's being done. The safety and well-being of people must never fall to the wayside during the push of the legalization of these medicines. What I mean by that is that we can never allow these acts to occur and sweep them under the rug because we are afraid that they may hurt the plant medicine movement. We must continue to advocate these medicines while also holding people accountable who consciously decide to misuse the medicine and their power as a facilitator. There is no place for this type of action, and it must be rooted out from all aspects of plant medicine if we are to successfully integrate them into our culture and into the collective healing. It's currently legal to administer Ayahuasca under certain church statuses in the United States. You will see churches under certain denominations allowed to be holding these ceremonies. Although they're a schedule one drug, like LSD and mushrooms, there are instances where it can legally be administered in the United States without the threat of punishment.

~ 3 ~

MECHANISM OF ACTION

Now I will move on to the mechanisms of action for the three compounds that I have been discussing so far in this book. Simply put, a mechanism of action is the actual physiological effect that the compound has on your body. If you are anything like me and you are a left-brained, logical thinker, that likes to know exactly how things work then this section is for you. You will notice that the mechanisms of action for the mushrooms, LSD, and the Ayahuasca are all generally the same, they just act in slightly different ways. The way that they interact with your body, specifically your brain, is that they mimic the serotonin neurotransmitter. To go a little further, it's the 5-HT2A serotonin receptor that these compounds mainly interact with. With LSD, it affects some additional receptors, but for the most part that 5-HT2A receptor is the one that's being affected the most. Let me give you a little background on what's happening in the brain so you can have a better idea of what's going on in there.

The brain works by sending signals between itself. You have a system to send these signals, which are long and thin with two distinct ends on them. One end sends the signals, and the other end receives them. There is a gap between these two points that separates them, which is called a synaptic gap. Just imagine you have two of your fingers pointed at one another and you hold them tip to tip with just a little bit of a gap in-between. That would represent both ends of your signal system and that synaptic gap in-between. The cells send signals across this gap via chemical messengers. These are called neurotransmitters. Some examples of these chemicals are dopamine, adrenaline, and serotonin. Neurotransmitters fire from the sending cell into the receptors of the receiving cell, thereby activating the receptors and then the receptors relay the message to the cell. Using the finger analogy again, an impulse will fire through the sending finger, then a neurotransmitter chemical goes through the gap between the fingers, that chemical goes into the receiving finger, and then that finger sends the message through like a message delivery system.

Each chemical has its own receptor which accommodates its shape, much like a lock and key does. A chemical that doesn't correspond to the shape of its receptor would not fit in it and therefore will not activate it. For example, a dopamine molecule won't activate a serotonin receptor because it doesn't fit, much like your front door key won't fit into your neighbor's lock. Certain psychoactive molecules activate the serotonin 5-HT2A receptor because they're very similar in structure to that serotonin molecule. They basically mimic and can open this doorway within your brain and allow your brain to connect in ways that it has not been connected before.

There is a massive influx of areas of the brain that are talking to one another that have not talked or typically don't talk in your normal waking consciousness. What does this mean for you? This means that you literally start to see your life from a completely different perspective. You see things in ways that you have never seen them before. You get out of our "DMN" or your default mode network. Your DMN is a word for your subconscious brain which accounts for up to 95% of your waking activity. It is your patterns, habits, and routines. In large, this makes up who you are and how you show up in the world. During these experiences, you can step away from your daily habits and see your life from a new and fresh perspective. This is what has such profound changes in your perspective and the way you are able to see yourself, your life, and the way you see the world.

Now you have a much firmer understanding of what is going on in your body as these compounds are taking their effect. There is a ton of misinformation that has been spread and taken as fact when it comes to these various psychedelics. One of these examples is people holding the belief that mushrooms are just food poisoning and that "tripping" is a person feeling the effects of this poisoning on our system. There are horror stories of people jumping out of windows and going back into their trips at random points in their life after the experience is over. That is why I feel it is so important to arm ourselves with a little bit of the knowledge of the science behind these experiences. It can help you in understanding these medicines and can also save you from having to go into these experiences with an added fear or what-if scenario that is not even plausible, to begin with. I am not saying that there is not any risk at all with these compounds because there are inherent risks and cautions that need to be taken. What I am saying is that these risks have been exacerbated and pushed as a fact to create fear around working with these substances for a questionable agenda.

Part 1: Pre-Ceremony

You now have some history of these medicines as well as some insights into how they interact with your body. Now I'm going to go on to talk about the portion of the experience that happens before the ceremony. Preparation for your psychedelic experience happens the moment that you make the decision to sit with the medicine and leads up until the actual ceremony and beyond. There is a wide range of things that you can consider when preparing for your experience to have you best prepared the day of. What I feel is so important about the things that I talk about, and really anything in life is that nothing is one size fits all. In this book, I share things that have worked for me or for others that I have come across in my reading and in my plant medicine work. It is important for you to read this information and take the time to feel into what resonates with you. Take what you feel is aligned with you and leave what you feel is not. This is not a book of rules telling you what you must do to have a good experience. This book is a guide that serves to offer tips, tricks, and routines that can potentially help you and your growth. If something does not feel right for you then there is nothing saying that you must use it. I am never here to sway someone's beliefs or prove that I am right. My only goal is to help others reach deeper levels of their own truth. Even if that truth is not congruent with mine, it is my wish that by sharing my perspective I can help others further solidify and have trust in their own knowledge and path. I cannot urge you enough, feel into what I share and only utilize what you feel is for your highest good.

~ 4 ~

AWARENESS

Awareness is such a crucial superpower to implement before the ceremony and in the integration work afterward. I break this concept down into three main pillars of awareness. These pillars will cover the areas in your life where it is most prevalent to shine awareness on. The three pillars are awareness of self, awareness of the environment, and awareness of the medicine. In this section, I will be providing questions to ask yourself that will help you to bring further awareness to these various areas.

Awareness of Self

<u>*Awareness of your traumas:*</u>

How have you been handling them?
How do they currently affect you?
Have you worked through them or do they weigh heavily?
What traumas have you been through
  (physical/sexual/emotional)?

Understanding your traumas and what you may be bringing to the experience can play an enormous role in how your experience plays out. This also plays a factor in how much resistance you have as things come up inside of the ceremonial experience. Often, you are moved towards facing some of the most difficult things in your life that you have spent a lifetime turning away from. If you are at least aware of what may come up this can take away a lot of the surprise that will only serve to be an added speed bump while inside of the ceremony space.

Awareness of your beliefs:

What are your belief systems like?
What are your beliefs about life, death, and spirituality?
What do you believe about the medicine you're going to be taking?
    Do you believe it's scary?
    Do you believe it's healing?
    Do you believe it's dangerous?
    Do you believe that it makes people go crazy?

You cannot hide from your belief systems inside of your plant medicine journey. These are all things that you are going to be bringing into the experience with you and can play an effect on how the experience plays out. Psychedelics have a powerful way of testing your belief systems and showing you things that may differ from what you currently believe. Your beliefs can project certain things onto your experience, and they have the power to bring about confusion and difficulty letting go. Having a loose grip on your beliefs with a sense of curiosity for the experience can help prevent you from holding on to old belief systems.

Having awareness of your thought patterns:

Are you nervous a lot of the time?
Are you anxious about a lot of things?
Are you typically optimistic or pessimistic?
Do you typically get lost in trains of thought?

Understanding these thought patterns going in will really give you some awareness of what may be coming up during the experience as well. Later I will be going into detail about the power of meditation and how that practice can be used to help with overactive thinking. Psychedelics tend to make the mind wander and there is the possibility to get lost in rabbit holes of thought and even paranoia. It is important to begin to cultivate the mind-body connection as early as possible so that you have practices in place to come back to center and not get lost in trains of thought.

Having awareness of your health:

How does your body typically feel?
Do you have pre-existing health conditions?
What does your physical health look and feel like?
What does your mental health look and feel like?

Knowing yourself both physically and mentally is very important and can potentially prevent something extreme from happening inside of the experience. The more physically prepared you can be, the better off you are because these experiences do take a physical toll on your body. The clearer that you can be with your vessel, the more easily you can move through these experiences and allow the medicine to work with you. Being aware of your mental health is extremely important as well. These medicines play an enormous role in your mental health. There are some red flags that I am going to discuss later to be aware of because while these substances have such a profound healing potential in them, they also have the potential to do some harm if you are in certain mental states and you are not taking the available precautions. Being aware of where you are physically and mentally is very crucial and cannot be overstated in this process.

Awareness of Environment

Awareness of your job:

Do you work with people you don't resonate with?
Are you working at a job that's really grinding you down?
Are you working at a place that ethically doesn't align with you?

Your job is a place where you spend most of your time throughout the week. You may be coming out of a psychedelic experience with some big, profound changes, and going back into certain job settings may prove to be very difficult. The psychedelic experience can really exacerbate that and really end up pushing you towards something different moving forward. Just having an awareness of how your job is, what your relationship is with your coworkers, and what kind of environment it is, can prove to be very beneficial for you.

Awareness of your housing situation:

Are you comfortable?
Is it a stable living condition?
Are you in a safe environment?
Are they aware of what's going on in your life?
Are you living with people that understand you?
Is there a chance you may be getting evicted or removed?

Having this stability at home is only going to help foster what's coming up and help foster the growth as you come through this experience. If you have instability at home and in your housing, it can be difficult to focus on and give energy to your healing process once getting back. Being aware of that before going into your experience is going to really help you on the backend with the integration work that is to come.

<u>*Awareness of your interpersonal relationships:*</u>

Do people understand what you're going through?
What kind of relationships do you have around you?
Do you have people in your life that are nonjudgmental?
Do you have people in your life that can hold space for you?
Do you have relationships with people that want to see you grow?

Understanding the friends and family of your life and how they're going to receive you, especially coming out of an experience like this, is very important. It is going to help build a support system around you. So many people get wrapped up in the lone wolf syndrome of feeling like they can and should tackle this all on their own. That is a difficult and lonely path. There are people that want to help you and to serve as that support system for you. It is so beneficial to begin to piece that system together beforehand rather than wait for moments where you are really in distress.

Awareness of the Medicine

Of course, if you are reading this book right now then you're putting in that work and I commend you for that. Everyone's experience is different, and your experience is going to be a bit different every single time you sit. But at least being aware of the experiences that may come up, reading some books, attending webinars, and just learning more about the effects other people are having and what may potentially come up will help you get a frame of reference for your experience. It can potentially help the experience and to help them make a little bit more sense rather than having no frame of reference at all, much like Albert Hoffman on his bicycle day.

Being aware of the dosages. This is very good to know, especially if you're deciding to journey with these medicines on your own. It is important to know that dosages are a rough baseline and can vary from person to person and even for yourself. A variety of factors can affect the impact a psychedelic has including set and setting, your diet, your intention, and what type of medicine you are taking. Even if someone else is giving you a dosage in a ceremony type of setting, arm yourself with knowledge and always be aware of what they are offering and in what dose. Again, you are your own best guru, and you know what is best for you deep down. Take the time to have this understanding so that you don't find yourself going deeper than anticipated and in a difficult spot that could have been avoided with a proper dose. A quote my wife said to me that has always stuck with me and that I think of every single time I take anything is "you can always take more, and you can never take less". This is a nice little reminder to replay for yourself before taking anything that has any sort of effect on your body, psychoactive or not.

Finally, it is great to know a bit about the history of the medicines. That's why I did a little bit of history at the beginning of this book. I think it's important to honor these medicines, where they've come from, the tribes that have used them, the ancestry that has used them, and just take some time to see where it comes from through the lineage. Psychedelics have been very demonized in recent culture and severely misunderstood. I think getting back to the roots, getting back to our ancestors and how they used this medicine helps us to tune more deeply into what's going on and what kind of relationship you can have with these various plants and compounds.

~ 5 ~

INTENTIONS

Now on to setting intentions for the experience. Setting intentions is a powerful practice that you will hear so many people talk about when it comes to preparing for your psychedelic journey. You can set your intentions going into a psychedelic medicine journey and even practice this daily. It is powerful to set intentions for your days, weeks, and even your life. I see intention as your opportunity to commune with the medicine and with the spirits of the medicine. It is an opportunity for you to send the message to the medicine saying, "Hey, listen, this is the part of me I want to be focusing on for this experience". This can be about what you want to work through or about a certain feeling you wish to explore. If I have learned anything working with plant medicines, it is that we don't always get what we want out of an experience, but we do always get what we need. Intention, however, allows you to create this kind of open dialogue between you and the medicine. I think that the medicine works with you, and this is reinforced if you take the time to communicate with it as well. It's a two-way street. Going in with intention allows you to speak to the things that you want to gain clarity on and to the things that you are feeling so this medicine can take that into account as you go through your experience. It helps to set a framework or a baseline for the experience.

I also believe that it primes you mentally for the experience. When you have this intention in your mind it is already primed up to the emotion, feeling, or whatever it is that you're calling to the surface. Your brain will already start to begin working through this or at least start to work with it. These intentions most certainly do not have to be set the day of the experience. I believe it's powerful to have it set out further than that. It could be days, weeks, and even months in advance. The further out you clarify your intention, the more you can better prepare yourself for the experience. Say you are looking to work through a certain trauma. You can begin to work with it beforehand and work with others beforehand, rather than possibly getting steamrolled during the experience and not being prepared mentally for what may come up and what that looks like. As I mentioned before, this whole experience starts long before you take the medicine. It can also really help to focus your awareness on your intention rather than getting caught up in the whole experience of the medicine. You can use the intention, especially if written down, to come back from various rabbit holes of thought that your mind may try to travel down.

It's important to note, try not to get caught up in a specific outcome. For example, having an intention of "I want to know what job I am meant to be doing" and setting this need to have to know that specific answer can set you up for a letdown. That is a specific outcome you are asking for. Rather than having that specific outcome, consider having the intention that sounds more like "my intention is to gain clarity around my career". The difference here is that you're not telling the medicine "Hey, I want you to tell me what my next move is". What I have learned is when I asked for direct answers like that, more times than not, I didn't get the direct answer. Often, what I did get was clarity or a certain kind of vision of the steps to be taken in a particular direction. Having a broader perspective from that manner allows more flexibility for the medicines to show you what you are meant to see without holding a certain expectation for the experience. With that being said, I am certainly not saying it is impossible to get a direct answer from your experience. I have certainly gone into experiences and even meditations with specific questions that I got specific answers for during the experience. I am not telling you to not have questions if you feel called to bring them into your experience. I just wanted to bring awareness to this so that you understand why a certain intention may have not yielded the outcome you had hoped. I have a couple of other examples of some powerful intentions that you can bring into your experience:

My intention is to learn to love my body.
My intention is to learn how to love myself.
My intention is for clarity on my life's purpose/career.
My intention is to learn how to accept and let go of my past.
My intention is to connect with myself and others more deeply.

These are just a couple of intentions that I have seen come up and yield some powerful results for people. Again, these aren't so much outcome-based. They are not saying "Hey, I want this answer, I need this answer". They are more so saying "This is an area that I feel a little lost in. I feel a little confused. How can you point me in the right direction here?" That is a very powerful way to step to these medicines with intentions, not get tied to a certain outcome, and be able to come away from the experience with something powerful to integrate that is tied to the intention which you brought in.

~ 6 ~

PRACTICES & ROUTINES

Now moving on to discussing regular practices and routines. I think it's very important to have regular practices before going into any type of visionary experience. While preparing to write this book an analogy came to me, and I think it's a powerful way to kind of envision why it's important to have regular practices before going into a plant medicine ceremony. Imagine you've never been in a car before. You have never traveled in a car, and you have never driven. You have never been in one period. Then, for your first time going for a ride in a car, you hop into a race car and that thing takes off going 200 plus miles an hour. That would probably scare most people straight. It would probably be a very terrifying experience.

Now imagine that you have driving experience of 20 or 30 years. Maybe you have a little bit of a lead foot, so you've done 100 maybe even 120 miles an hour in the car a time or two. So now you have some prior frame of reference to driving and being in a car at higher rates of speed. Maybe you've never been in a sports car going 180 or 200 before, but you've at least been in the car going some amount of speed that is remotely close to that. I feel like it's the same thing with the visionary experience. We go into a psychedelic trip and sometimes it very much feels like we are going 200 plus miles an hour, getting thrown around both mentally and physically. If you have some regular practices, then these can be the things that allow you to better handle that 200 mile an hour experience. Now that's not to say that that fast experience or that psychedelic experience is going to be easy because it still has the potential to be a bit scary at times. It's still going to be that fast experience. But if you have something to fall back onto and you have prior experiences moving into it then you will be better equipped to handle that experience in a more composed way.

That's why I think it's important to have regular practices that facilitate this rapid change in your consciousness. I'm going to talk about four practices in this book that have had the biggest direct correlation to the psychedelic experience for me. There's certainly more that can be utilized, but these are the four that have been most prevalent in my journey.

First, you have meditation. Meditation is something that's become somewhat of a hot topic, especially in Western cultures over the past couple of decades. There's a lot of different definitions of meditation, types of meditation, and uses of meditation. At the core of the practice, it is aimed to help us develop a deeper and more cohesive relationship with our brain and thoughts. I don't believe it's always about shutting our minds off or just making our minds go blank. Rather, it's about cultivating a relationship with your mind. I don't think any part of us is something to be shunned away, pushed away, or shut off. As thoughts come up and want to race around in your head it is your opportunity to detach from those thoughts and to watch them go by but not jump in and engage with them.

A lot of people refer to the analogy of saying that your thoughts are like a river just floating by. If you don't jump in the river of thought then you don't get swept away and taken downstream. Another great analogy for your stream of thoughts is envisioning a busy highway. All the cars passing by are your individual thoughts. If you allow the thoughts to just go by, without jumping in the passenger seat and going for the ride, then you are becoming the awareness behind the thoughts. That is where you are now cultivating that relationship with your mind. You are not fighting it or telling it to be any certain type of way. You are just becoming the observer of the thoughts and not allowing your consciousness to be pulled away as those thoughts come and go. You may jump in the river or hop in the passenger seat from time to time and that is just fine. From there, you just become aware of what you have done and come back to a place of awareness, and begin again. Just like going to the gym to work out other muscles of your body, each repetition of this will strengthen your ability to not get lost in the stream of thoughts that occupy your mind countless times in a day. This skill is going to be very powerful, especially in a psychedelic state where your mind may be racing into all different areas of thought. Having that meditation practice to fall back on can be a powerful way to re-center and move away from the various rabbit holes that may come up during your experience. Trying to figure this out on the day of the experience with no prior practice may be much more difficult to implement. Therefore, implementing this practice well before your intended experience can prove to be very beneficial for you.

Next, you have a yoga practice. Yoga also helps with control of the mind as well as assisting in energy movement throughout your body. These psychedelic experiences cause a lot of energy to come up and this energy wants to move through you in these experiences. This is something that is prevalent in a lot of psychedelic journeys. Having this practice to fall back on and having these movements in your toolbox can be very beneficial during some of the most difficult times during your experience. Sometimes it takes something more than just a mental practice to move through the experience. Sometimes it takes the movement of these stagnant energies that have been stored in your body so that you may allow them to be released. Yoga is a powerful way to be able to do this. Any type of movement can really have a powerful and transformative effect as well. Ecstatic dance can be a powerful practice that you can tap into during these experiences also. Having a regular practice that gets you comfortable with the movement and comfortable with how it feels to move energy around your body will pay dividends during your experience. There is no particular way this needs to look, so have fun exploring and trying on different types of movement that feel right for you. There are plenty of practices and modalities to explore and work with. Some may resonate more than others so don't get discouraged if you are struggling to find a practice that feels right for you. Toss on some of your favorite music one day when nobody is home and see the different ways in which your body wants to move around!

Journaling is another powerful way for you to get in the practice of quite literally getting out of your head. It is an opportunity for you to become more aware of your thoughts and emotions on a more consistent basis. Taking the time to get out of your head and getting that onto paper is a powerful practice. It is a great habit to get into, especially once you get into your integration work. Having this regular practice beforehand will be something that you will really want to tap into later during your journeys and then also in your integration work. While journaling is commonly done in a notebook of some sort there is nothing saying that this cannot be done through voice notes on the computer or phone. Again, this is about making routines and habits that work best for you and have the lowest barrier of entry. The point of the practice is the reflection and taking the time to become aware of your thoughts, feelings, and habits. If this works best for you in audio form, then lean into that and make that work for you. There is no set framework that you must follow to be properly journaling. I journal daily and each day looks a bit different to me. Some days I recap the day and others it may be about a particular emotion or situation that I felt I needed to write about. Other days I may just be inspired to write a poem or do a drawing. As with everything, listen to your intuition and do what feels right for you. You are your own best guru, and your inner intelligence will guide you to the ways that are most beneficial for you at that moment.

The final practice I feel called to discuss is leaning on others for support. I don't necessarily mean this in terms of having a life coach, counselor, or therapist. These are all amazing avenues of support, but it could also just be a friend or family member that you confide in and that you get super vulnerable with. The key here is just getting comfortable with leaning on others and not feeling like you must tackle everything alone. I do men's retreats and men's work through various workshops and events and one of the common themes that we're always coming across is men that have what I call the "lone wolf syndrome". Now women certainly experience this as well, but as I mentioned, my history is mainly doing men's work. That "lone wolf syndrome" that both men and women get is the mentality that says, "'I have done it this far on my own, I don't need help from anyone". This ends up holding you back from wanting to be vulnerable with others. I have seen first-hand, the power in people coming together, whether it's men or women, in vulnerability and leaning on one another for support. Many times, we think we're a burden to other people, but the fact is that people love to help, and people want you to come to them for support. If they don't want you to come to them for support then that's not the person you should be going to for support in the first place.

It feels good to help. We all know that feeling of when we give a gift or make someone feel good. How good that feels and how much that fills our cup. So, allow people to step into that role for you. Allow people to be there for you and I can promise you the healing that will come from it really compounds your healing moving forward. When you close off and don't allow others to be there for you then you are robbing them of the opportunity to be there for you in a way that will make them feel good. It is a two-way street of healing that can benefit all the parties involved. This is such a powerful practice to use, especially before going through your psychedelic journey. Psychedelic experiences may be confusing, disorienting, and sometimes hard to make meaning of. Being able to talk to people that understand the experience, maybe not specifically yours, but at least the psychedelic space can make your integration much easier to work through. Another person having some understanding of what's going on with you is going to be so pivotal to you not feeling like you're alone in what you're going through. The fact is that you're not. Many other people are going through these experiences, and they want to be there alongside you to support, uplift and be there as a system for you to lean on as you go through your process. Building this support system from scratch on the back end of your experience can serve as just another speed bump in the road as opposed to already having this system in place prior to going into your experience. Try not to get caught up in the "lone wolf syndrome" and see the massive shifts it makes in your growth in healing.

~ 7 ~

DIET

The final part I am going to talk about, regarding before the journey, is your diet. When I talk about diet, I'm not just talking about what you are eating. Your diet is much more than that. It is about all the external stimuli that come into your awareness and body at any given moment. So yes, it's what you eat, but it's also what and who you interact with. The things that you watch and the things that you listen to. All this external stimulus influences you, whether that's on a conscious or an unconscious level. Really being aware of that is very important, especially in the days and weeks leading up to a psychedelic experience. First, what are you eating? Being as clean as possible with eating only proves to help with the experience and to help with your connection to the medicine. If your body is in a state of detox and you have a lot of things clogging you up, along with a lot of toxins within your body, then the medicine is going to be working through that additional barrier. You can envision it as this foggy layer that can serve to inhibit your experience to varying degrees. Having the cleanest possible vessel as you move into these experiences is only going to help you in the end. It is only going to help deepen that connection.

When you go into Ayahuasca ceremonies there is typically a "dieta" protocol that is followed for the participants. I've seen these outlined for 15 days, 30 days, and beyond. There are different guidelines, procedures, and recommendations based upon who you talk to and the culture that you are working with. I'm with the belief that you know what's best for you when you are really tuned in and connected to your body. Your body knows how and what will respond best for you. You must be careful though because this knowledge can easily be distorted by various cravings that come from certain emotional responses or food addictions that are causing this distortion. With that being said, the common restrictions that we see on these dietas are the restrictions of caffeine, oils, sugar, alcohol, fermented foods, yeast, red meat, pork, dairy, spicy foods, and marijuana. As I mentioned, this is not a fully exhaustive list. There are certainly more items that can and have been included on this list and some of the items from that list may be deemed as ok to certain cultures also. Always seek to be in tune with yourself and with your body. Listen to it. Listen to what it's saying through your stomach and the way you feel before and after eating certain foods. Your body's always talking to you. Just be very aware of yourself, be aware of what people are doing, take that into account, and then use that knowledge to best prepare yourself physically for what's going to be going on during these experiences.

Your diet also includes being mindful of what you're watching, what you're reading, and what you are listening to. This includes television, social media, radio, the people you are around, and the types of material that you are consuming. This is the great age of information and the great age of disinformation. There's so much turbulence going on in the world and so much fear being perpetuated. There are a lot of intense things happening and we cannot blatantly deny that fact. But what are you allowing in? What are you constantly watching? This is especially important in the days and weeks leading up to your psychedelic experience. If you're going into a ceremony having just consumed a lot of fear-based information then this can absolutely influence your mental state, which in turn influences your experience. Having a detox from the things that may affect you in that way can be very beneficial. There is a chance that your experience is going to be all tied up and with the collective fears of these things that you've been allowing into your consciousness, rather than the internal work that you need to be going through. Your internal traumas, fears, and whatever may need to come up for you may take a backseat to this collective energy that is now swirling around in your consciousness.

I think it's all divine. What you get from an experience is always going to be what you need to get but being aware of what you are allowing in will just help guide you to your own internal healing and possibly not entail healing of things that are external to you. If you are bringing those external things into the experience, then maybe that is just the lesson you are meant to have for that journey. As I said, you can take active steps to help your process, but you can never be wrong. In the end, it is all working towards your growth and development in one way or another. The last part of your diet to be mindful of is who you are connecting with. Are you having positive, wholesome interactions? Or are you constantly having stressful, angering interactions? Is there a lot of resistance with those in your life that are saying you're crazy for doing this and they are being judgmental because of their biases and beliefs? This can cause difficulty in the integration process as well as bring a level of guilt, shame, and self-doubt going into the experience. These are all things that you may carry into the experience and make them more difficult to navigate. The psychedelic experience already has its own potential built-in struggles and difficulties, so dealing with shame and dealing with those relationships on top of it is only going to put added stress on there for you to deal with. This will only serve to exacerbate your struggles and make the integration process that much more difficult.

Try to surround yourself with people that support your decision to journey. Building that support system before you go in is important because then you're going to have it as you come out of it and it's going to be in place waiting for you. Having people that understand you and understand the work that you're going through and who generally support you is going to be very beneficial. This is a core human desire, a core human need. To be connected, to be understood, to be loved, and to be heard. These are needs that are very basic to all human beings. Begin to tend to that core human desire as early as possible and your growth will continue at such an exponential rate moving forward.

Before I get into the during ceremony portion, I have some important questions for you to ponder in three different categories. I have broken them down into personal, medicines, and health-related questions. Again, these are not all-inclusive lists. There are more questions you can be thinking about, but I found these to be the most prevalent for me and my clients as we prepare for our visionary experience.

~ 8 ~

REFLECTION QUESTIONS

This section will be outlining some powerful questions for you to think about as you prepare for an upcoming plant medicine experience. I have broken the questions down into three categories which are personal, medicine, and health. The personal questions have to do with your mindset and emotions. The medicine questions are geared toward the plant medicine you are sitting with and developing a deeper relationship with them going into the experience. Finally, the health questions revolve around your physical and mental health leading up to the experience. No matter how much experience you have, it is always important to reflect on these various areas before we decide to sit with the medicine. This can be done in a journaling exercise, with a partner, or with yourself. You are a different person every time you journey with plant medicines so these questions will continually be relevant for you to think about before your ceremony.

Personal Questions to Ponder

Why am I interested in exploring this medicine?
Am I trying to escape a current emotion or feeling?
How am I preparing my set and setting?
How will I be tying up any loose ends?
    Do I have to complete any work?
    Do I need to get a sitter for my kids or animals?
    Who do I have to inform?

What is my support system during the experience?
What do I know about the substance being taken?
   Are there any safety precautions to consider?
   What are my beliefs or fears around the psychedelic experience?

Why am I interested in exploring the medicine? Is it more for a healing experience or more for a recreational purpose? The purpose behind my psychedelic experiences has certainly shifted over the years. At the beginning of my journey, my intentions were deeply focused on the healing of my unresolved traumas and pains. As I began to do my healing and integration work, my relationship with the medicines began to shift and evolve. While these medicines hold an enormous capacity to help us heal, they also allow us to learn about ourselves in a deeper way and from a new perspective. Sometimes I turned to the medicine to break out of a pattern that I was having difficulty moving away from. Sometimes I worked with them to gain inspiration and insight for my creative endeavors. You don't have to feel obligated to have a particular interest in the medicine, but it is important to be aware of your interests and why you are feeling called to take them.

Am I trying to escape a current emotion or feeling going into this experience? If there is a certain emotion or feeling that you are trying to run from then there is a very likely chance that the medicine will flip you 180 degrees and turn you right back into the thing that you are seeking to avoid. Psychoactive compounds are not a way to get away from the things that cause us pain. They do not have a numbing effect like some other drugs do. That is because the way to move beyond your pains is to move through them and not away from them. This can be a scary concept to comprehend but on the other end of this pain is liberation from it and the stranglehold it may have on your consciousness.

How am I preparing my set and setting? I will be going into the set (mindset) and setting (location) in more detail later in this book. To start, how are you preparing your mind and how are you preparing the space that you will have the experience in? If you are not going somewhere for a guided experience, then what are you doing to make your space as conducive to healing as possible for you? It cannot be stressed enough how big of a role that set and setting play in how your experience plays out. There is an interplay between the medicine, its effects, and your set and setting.

How will I be tying up any loose ends? If there are loose ends that you have not tied up before your experience, then they may take up your mental space during your experience. As I mentioned earlier, your mind may be racing all over the place during your journey. This can have a very therapeutic effect but if there are a lot of things on your mind not relating to your internal world then this can serve to distract you. Make sure you get all your work done. Make sure you let people know where you are and that they will not be hearing from you. Make sure you have a reliable sitter that confirms with you and that you trust with your kids or pets. This will reduce the mental strain that you may experience.

What is my support system during the experience? Are you in a guided ceremony, are you with friends, or are you alone? It is always recommended to have a guide or sitter on site with you in case of difficulties that may arise. If you feel called to journey alone then it can be beneficial to, at a minimum, have people that know what you are doing, will be readily available and can come to support you if need be. I will discuss facilitators in more detail later but for now, just be aware of the support system you have in place and what feels good for you. While you may be comfortable in the plant medicine space, you never quite know what may come up for you. This is regardless of how many times you have explored these states of consciousness before.

What do I know about the substance being taken? Do you understand the history, dosages, effects, and safety precautions that may be required for what you are taking? This can be lifesaving information, especially the understanding of the various contraindications with prescription medications. Being on particular prescription medication and coupling that with a particular psychedelic substance can yield potentially life-threatening effects that will be discussed in greater detail in further chapters.

What are my beliefs or fears around the psychedelic experience? You will be bringing all your beliefs, fears, and judgments into the space with you. There has been a lot of false stigmas spread around psychedelics and much of this misinformation has been taken as fact by society. If you go into an experience with fear and think that these substances make people go crazy and that you may jump out of a window, then that may manifest in your experience. Take a hard look at your beliefs around what these substances can do to you and for you.

Medicine Questions to Ponder

What have been my past experiences with visionary medicines?
What techniques can I use to get through difficult emotions?
How can I deepen my relationship with the medicine?
Explore writing a letter to the medicine:
  What would I like to say to it or ask it?
  What would I like from it?
Write down reminders for yourself to reflect on:
  IE: breath, this will pass, surrender, go with the flow, allow

What have been my past experiences with visionary medicines? Reflecting on your past visionary experiences can help prepare you for what may be coming up now and what type of experience you may have. This is certainly not a guarantee. Your psychedelic experience can vary greatly from one time to another, but this does not mean it hurts to reflect on your prior experiences and use any insights from those times in your upcoming journey. If you have no prior experience, it can be beneficial to talk with people who have had prior experiences and hear their perspectives. It can be beneficial to have a frame of reference going into the experience rather than trying to make full sense of everything as it is happening.

What techniques can I use to get through difficult emotions? We talked earlier about having regular routines to fall back on if things get turbulent throughout your experience. Think about some of the techniques that have some of the greatest effects on you and your emotional stability. This can be a powerful breathwork exercise, a certain meditation practice, or a series of yoga moves. Having this planned beforehand can help keep it at the forefront of your mind as you navigate some of the choppier waters of your experience.

How can I deepen my relationship with the medicine? When you decide to sit with the various medicines you are forming a bond and creating a relationship with them. This process starts before you even put that substance into your body. How do you feel that you can deepen that relationship? I will tell you, just by reading this book and learning more you are cultivating that deeper relationship. You can also speak to the medicine through prayer, writing, and meditation. These can be powerful ways to deepen that bond and allow you to receive all the messages that you are meant to receive from them.

Explore writing a letter to the medicine: I really enjoy this exercise before working with a certain type of visionary or non-visionary substance. Writing a letter to the medicine helps to personify it and allows us to continue to create that deeper connection with it. It is my belief that all plants and medicines have a spirit or an essence that is associated with them. It is these spirits that we commune with and that work with us to guide our healing. I mentioned before that we don't always get what we want from an experience, but we always get what we need. I see this relationship as a 2-way street. The more of an effort you take to make your intentions known the more the medicine can work with those intentions and meet you in your healing.

Write down reminders for me to reflect on during the trip: Even if you have a facilitator or a guide with you it can be powerful to have a sheet of notes from your past self. These notes can be things to remember or actions to take that will help you get through the difficulty. Sometimes just a simple reminder to "let go" or "breathe" can be all it takes to allow you to move through the difficulty you are facing. This may seem very simple, but it is a very powerful and useful practice to utilize.

Health Questions to Ponder

Do I have any health issues that may be aggravated?
Do I currently suffer from any mental health issues?
Am I currently taking any mental health medication?
Have I been hospitalized for any mental health issues in the past?
Am I currently having any physical or mental emergencies?
Am I in overall good health both physically and mentally?

Do I have any health issues that may be aggravated? I mentioned that the psychedelic experience can be intense both physically and mentally. Being aware of pre-existing and underlying health conditions is pivotal as you prepare to move forward with your experience. Later in the book, I will discuss the red flags and contraindications for these medicines so you will have a better understanding of the precautions that may need to be taken before you dive in.

Do I currently suffer from any mental health issues? While these medicines hold enormous power for healing our psyche, they do also come with some risks so they should never be taken lightly. If you suffer from severe mental health issues and certain mental health diagnoses, then extreme caution should be taken. While these medicines have been shown to be a breakthrough treatment, there have been cases of people coming out on the other side of an experience in a worse condition than when they went in. These powerful substances can expand the mind in incredible ways but a mind that is not ready for that type of expansion can suffer some undesirable consequences if the person is not careful. Therefore, it is important to be aware of your mental state and always consult professional guidance if you are unsure about the risks involved for you.

Am I currently taking any mental health medication? This is an extremely important thing to consider and let your sitter or guide know about before going into your experience. As we discussed earlier, these various compounds interact with the neurons and receptors in your brain. This is very similar in the way that the most common mental health medication and antidepressants work as well. The result of these two substances working together in your body can have results that vary from canceling one another out to more life-threatening effects. Always be completely honest with yourself and with whoever is administering the medicine because it can be a very serious issue that arises if you are not.

Have I been hospitalized for any mental health issues in the past? Take some time to reflect on any past mental health history that you may have had. It can be easy to lock parts of our memory away and never look back at them. If you have been hospitalized in the past for mental health, then this can serve as an important reminder of something that may still be prevalent for you to some degree. Just because you have been hospitalized for a mental health issue does not mean that you shouldn't explore the medicine or that you are broken by any means. Just use this question to explore your history and reflect on the progress you have made since then. This may also help you with setting your intention for the experience.

Am I currently having any physical or mental emergencies? You may have signed up for your experience weeks, months, and even a year in advance. Some of these experiences cost thousands of dollars and we invest a lot to partake in them with the hopes of healing and growth. You may have been in the state to explore the medicine at the time that you signed up but what has happened between then and now? Just because you have committed to the experience does not mean that you must follow through and that following through is the best decision. This can be a hard truth to face but it is so important, to be honest with yourself about what your current physical and emotional state is. You can always reschedule. The medicine will always be there waiting for you when you are ready.

Am I in overall good health both physically and mentally? Finally, just do an overall check of your physical and mental health. Take note of any physical ailments and pains that may be coming up for you. Take note of your emotional state and emotional stability. The more confident you feel in your physical and emotional state than the more you will set yourself up for success in the experience. Awareness is such a critical superpower to employ and will allow you to understand areas in your life that you may want to focus on as you move forward with your intentions and letter to the medicine.

~ 9 ~

JOURNEY CHECKLIST

Journey Checklist

- ☐ Water
- ☐ Test Kit
- ☐ Comfortable Clothing
- ☐ Intentions
- ☐ Healthy Food / Snacks
- ☐ Fruit
- ☐ Important Numbers
- ☐ Plan For Dificulty
- ☐ Yoga Mat
- ☐ Crystals

- ☐ Cell Phone Off / Silent
- ☐ Music
- ☐ Sitter / Guide
- ☐ Tissues
- ☐ Instruments
- ☐ Art Supplies
- ☐ Journal
- ☐ Meaningful Items
- ☐ Diffuser / Oils
- ☐ Rapé / Mapacho
- ☐ Smudge / Scents
- ☐ Other:

Here is a journey checklist that I have put together for you to reference for any upcoming psychedelic experiences. This doesn't include everything that you could potentially have with you, but these are some things that I have found extremely beneficial in having with me for my experiences. Planning beforehand will save you frustration and difficulty later on. It is best to be as prepared as possible to ease the mental stressors that may impact you during your experience.

Water: You always want to make sure you stay hydrated. There is a lot of energy moving around and you may find yourself sweating and moving around a lot. For this reason, it can be easy to get dehydrated quickly so always have water readily available to you.

Test Kit: Having a test kit is important, especially if you are exploring a substance by yourself or with friends. If you can afford to buy these medicines and have these experiences, then you can afford to test them. This is especially true with the LSD as there have been some different variations coming out that are not fully LSD. You just want to be careful. You want to always test and ensure you know what you are getting and where you are getting it from. The intention behind the medicine, who prepares it, how it's prepared, and the love and intention that go into it play a role in the experience that you ultimately have.

Comfortable Clothing: You want to make sure that you are comfortable throughout your experience, and this includes your clothing as well. You don't want to be constricted in any way and it is best to be as comfortable as possible, whatever that looks and feels like to you.

Intentions: We talked about intentions earlier in the book. Bring those intentions with you either in your mind or on paper so that you can hold them with you during your experience.

Healthy Food/Snacks: Ensure that you have healthy food and snacks in place, especially after your journey is over. The hunger typically doesn't hit during the peak phases of the experience but afterward, you can be depleted after going through so much. You're going to want some healthy foods and snacks to replenish yourself with. Pre-planning snacks beforehand will help you to replenish your body with good nutrients instead of having to figure something out and potentially eating things that may not be best for your body. I will say from experience that fruit tastes so incredible afterward, so have some of your favorite fruits on hand waiting for you. I promise you will thank me for that one.

Important numbers: We talked about having a support system in place and having important numbers written down can be very beneficial. Technology can be very difficult at times when you are on a psychedelic. Writing these important numbers down can be just a little bit easier to manage and to connect with if you should need to use them during a time of difficulty. There are also easy-to-use apps that you can download that have the psychedelic text and call support at the simple click of a button.

Plan For Difficulty: Already having a plan in place if something should happen can save a lot of stress and anguish during your experience. Having a phone number, a certain room, a certain song, or anything that you feel can help to ground and recenter yourself. This can help give you an ease of mind going in and a plan to fall back on in the heat of the moment.

Yoga mat: You may want to stretch out, do some yoga, and partake in some stretching exercises. A yoga mat can come in handy, especially if your space has a hard surface. This mat can also serve as a reminder to you of one of the various tools available in your experience.

Crystals: It's always great to have some crystals around. They can be a powerful way for you to help ground and center. Different crystals have different energetic frequencies that ultimately influence your energetic body. Having them around and making yourself an altar can help as you navigate through difficult times in your experience.

Cell Phone Off/Silent: Have your cell phone off, on silent, or on airplane mode. All it takes is one message or one phone call to throw your journey in a completely different direction. One thing can throw you into a tailspin that may be difficult to get out of. It is suggested to have that cell phone away, have it silenced, and have it in a place where you will not see it and be distracted from the inner work that you are doing.

Music: Having music available is very important. Music can be a powerful tool to help guide your experience and to help move the energy throughout your time. It is common to utilize music that ascends and descends throughout the experience. This process aims to align with the energy of your experience as you go through the come up, peak, and comedown phases of your journey.

Facilitator/Guide: It is always going to be recommended for there to be a facilitator or a guide present for any experience. There are there to help as your grounding presence and for with anything that may come up. I am going to talk more about facilitators and guides along with what exactly their role is later in this book.

Tissues: Sometimes you will do some heavy releasing in your experience. This can be crying, sweating, a runny nose, and anything along those lines. Having tissues can be helpful for you to avoid some messes and ensure you are not using those comfy clothes as your rag.

Music Instruments/Art Supplies: Sometimes you may want to just express. Energy may want to come through you in a creative outlet. Having some instruments and art supplies handy will be helpful if this should be the case. It may be difficult to verbalize what you are feeling or going through at certain points. Creative outlets serve as a way for you to express these feelings and emotions in a more abstract kind of way.

Journal: Having a journal handy, and with some prompts ready, will make it easily accessible for you to write down what you are experiencing. Sometimes getting out of your head and getting things onto paper can help you along your way. Just the act of writing can allow you to come to some new and profound realizations. We will be coming back to journaling later in the integration portion of the book.

Meaningful Items: Something to you that can be helpful during the experience and means something to you. This can be a picture, stuffed animal, blanket, pillow, or anything else that you feel would bring you comfort in a time of need.

Diffuser/Oils: Smells can play a big part in your experience. These experiences are happening with all your senses put together. Having smells can help you to ground and clear your mind in times of struggle. If there is a particular smell that you really enjoy then make sure to have that with you so that you can lean on it when needed. Even if you don't have a diffuser, just a sniff of essential oil from the bottle can go a long way.

Rapé/Mapacho: These two popular tobacco blends have powerful effects. Rapé is a nasal snuff tobacco blend and mapacho is a smoked tobacco blend. I will talk about that a little bit more later and explain how they can help you in the releasing process.

Smudges/Scents: Utilizing different smudges like Sage and Palo Santo helps to clear energies in the room. It can be beneficial to use these before the experience to create a fresh space, energetically, for you to work in. Also, any other incense or scents that you find beneficial you can utilize as well. If you are in a group setting be mindful of others around you, because something that helps you can be bothersome for others. It is important to discuss this beforehand so that nobody is suddenly overcome by a sudden smell that takes over a space.

This is my journey checklist and like I said it doesn't necessarily include everything you could possibly have, but this is a great baseline for creating a conducive environment for as best of an experience as possible for you. I will now be getting into the red flag conditions to watch out for before deciding to sit with a particular medicine.

~ 10 ~

RED FLAGS

Before getting into talking about the during-ceremony portion of the book, it is important to discuss some red flags and proceed with cautions. This is a topic that can and does have whole books written about them. I am going to be going over some of the most common red flags that you want to be on the lookout for before moving forward with your psychedelic experience. It is always advised to consult a medical professional if you are unsure of the risks associated with your physical or mental conditions. This list includes but is not limited to:

An unstable or acute mental health issue
Addiction conditions/active withdrawal
Severe Traumas (Physical, Sexual, Emotional)
PTSD symptoms
Physical medical conditions:
    Heart conditions
    High blood pressure
Current or prior diagnosis of:
    Bipolar disorder
    Schizophrenia
    Paranoia
    Personality Disorder
Severe Depression
Suicidal/Self-Harming Thoughts
High anxiety/panic attacks

Poor regulation of emotions
Neurological disorders
Use of antidepressants
Eternal Pessimism
No support system

While the medicine has the power to help you work through these conditions, they also hold the potential to exacerbate them and make them worse. Therefore, the use of awareness and caution is pivotal for both the participant and the guide when it comes to ensuring mental stability for you.

These are red flags and I tell you to proceed with caution, but it doesn't necessarily mean that you cannot take psychedelic medicines at all. In the clinical trials being conducted right now, for many of these conditions, if you answer yes on the questionnaire then you will be automatically rejected from that trial. That does not mean that this is not an option for you altogether. For me specifically, I checked the boxes of severe trauma, PTSD, severe depression, suicidal thoughts, and substance abuse. There were a lot of red flags within my psyche as I began to explore plant medicines. Looking back, I wish I knew back then what I know now. I sure would have taken more precautions as I explored these altered states of consciousness. But ultimately, the medicines helped me to move through my struggles and really turn my life and my mental state around in such a big way. I personally believe and have experienced firsthand that these medicines can help us move through intense mental health struggles in ways that modern therapy can only scratch the surface.

Your mental health struggles and "disorders" don't mean you are not a candidate for using these tools to your advantage. It does mean that you should proceed with caution, really have the support systems in place, the guides in place, and the professionals in place to help you ensure that you are doing it safely. If you don't take caution, it can send you down a path that's not ultimately healing and will leave you on the other end more confused, more hurt, and more fragmented than when you started. I believe that it is up to the individual to tune into what is best for them and to consult professionals, especially if they have a history of health complications. Also, I want to touch on SSRI medications. SSRI (Selective Serotonin Reuptake Inhibitor) medications are typically used as antidepressants in the treatment of major depressive and anxiety disorders. Put simply, they don't allow the serotonin to re-uptake into your system. As we talked about before, the main mechanism of action for these various psychedelics is mimicking the serotonin receptor chemicals within the brain. This combination can lead to a wide range of undesirable effects occurring.

The effects of this combination can range from the substances canceling one another out all the way up to having potentially life-threatening effects for the participant. Serotonin syndrome is one of these potentially lethal effects, which occurs when there is an over-accumulation of serotonin in the body. Being hypervigilant of the medications you are on and being honest with yourself and the facilitator is of utmost importance in this process. There are charts that contain various prescription and non-prescription medications along with how they interact with psychoactive compounds. These charts allow you to see the risks associated as well as the amount of time you may need to detox before it is safe to move forward with a psychedelic journey. Never play the guessing game with this, it is like playing Russian roulette and your life is worth more than that. I always keep a copy of this contraindication guide handy so that I am always aware of potential complications that may arise for me or my clients. This does not necessarily have to be prescription medication also, so just be aware that there are over-the-counter medicines included in this list as well. If you ever have any doubts at all, please seek the guidance of someone who understands the risks and can help point you in the right direction. There are plenty of resources and groups that are ready to provide you with assistance and ensure your safety.

Part 2:
During-Ceremony

Now that you understand how to physically, mentally, and emotionally prepare for your psychedelic experience it is time to get into the during ceremony portion of this book. The visionary experience is unique to every individual and you can never fully know what to expect each time you sit in a ceremony. You can, however, arm yourself with knowledge and tools which you can implement through the various stages of your journey. In this section, I will be going over some things you can look out for, what you may potentially experience, as well as some techniques that you can utilize to get you through any difficulties that may arise in your experience. It is important to not go into these experiences with any expectations but that doesn't mean it is not important to bring awareness to what may potentially come up for you. This awareness can prove very beneficial for you as you are navigating the sometimes turbulent waters of the psychedelic experience.

~ 11 ~

DOSAGES

Now that you have prepared for your experience and you have a firm understanding of the red flags as well as risks associated, it is time to move on to the during ceremony portion of the book. To start off this section I am going to be going over some generic dosages of the three psychedelics I have been talking about in this book. Be aware that these are just general guidelines. They will give you a rough outline of the dosages and the effects they will have but it can vary from person to person. This can fluctuate based upon diet, experience, mindset, and a plethora of different factors that can influence how these dosages affect you. I know personally, for me, I have had a three-gram dose of mushrooms that felt much heavier than a five-gram dose. It is just depending on the strain, where I was mentally at the time, what I had been eating, as well as my set and setting. While these guidelines can give you a good outline, just be aware that the dosages can vary from person to person and even from time to time for the same person

First, I will go over the doses of psilocybin mushrooms. At the lower end of the dosage chart is your micro-dosing amount. That is going to typically be 0.1 to 0.3 grams of dried mushrooms. A microdose is something that is utilized on a more consistent basis, and it has no psychedelic side effects. The point of this dosage is to get the neurological effects without having the psychological effects. Neuroscience now shows that you have the ability for neurogenesis. What this means is that you can regenerate neural connections that have been lost, which for a long time it was believed is not possible. People will do this in varying schedules at the rate of three to four times a week. It is not suggested to take this microdose amount every day because you will eventually build a tolerance to it and see diminishing returns on the effects. With this practice, you are allowing your brain to begin to talk between the different areas in new ways which will enable you to create new habits, patterns, and routines more easily. As we discussed earlier when you take a macro-dose (large dose) your brain lights up with new connections all throughout the brain. The thing is that after that dose, your brain eventually goes back to a baseline where old patterns and connections will start to come back. The microdose allows you to slowly make and keep those new connections that will last over time when used in conjunction with your integration practices.

Next, you have a half gram to a gram dose, which is referred to as a creative dose. Artists and creatives have been known to take these doses as it helps to open the creative portals inside them. It aids in creativity but is still below a psychoactive dose. You are not really getting visuals at this point, but you will be feeling an increase in creativity and inspiration. From there you can move up to a one-to-two-gram dose. Now you are looking at what can be considered a "moderate" dose. At this amount, you can start to have some heavier types of experiences, including the introduction of some visuals as well. Depending on the strain and your diet you can possibly experience an intense trip at this level. From this point, you will start to get into heavier doses. Three to five grams are at the dosage for some heavy perceptual distortion, more intense visuals, and the possibility of ego dissolution. The ego dissolution experience that I discussed earlier in this book occurred on a 3.5-gram dose. A common threshold dose you will hear spoken about is an ⅛. An ⅛ refers to 3.5 grams or 1/8th of an ounce. As I mentioned before, I've had some three-gram journeys that felt more intense than five-gram journeys and vice versa. In this realm, you are at the strong end of the spectrum, and you are going to be feeling it both perceptually and visually. Finally, you have what's known as a heroic dose, which is a dosage of five-plus grams. This is only recommended for the experienced psychonaut, and it is recommended to have a sitter, guide, or support system in place for this type of experience. At this level, people report the complete dissolution of their sense of self, feeling interconnected to everything, and becoming disconnected from their sense of reality at times. While this can sound scary, many report this to be a liberating and life-changing experience. Again, an experience like this for a mind that is not ready can be a very traumatizing experience. It is important to go at your pace, at your comfort, and listen to your intuition always.

Next, you have the dosages for LSD which is measured in UG or micrograms. A microgram is equivalent to one-millionth of a gram. As you can see LSD has a much lower dosage amount than the psilocybin mushroom category. For LSD, the micro-dosing amount is going to be measured at the 10 to 50 microgram range. The creative dose is going to be at the 50 to 100 microgram doses. Your threshold, or moderate dose, is going to be coming in at the 100 to 150 microgram range. This is where you will have changes in perception, visuals, and the potential for ego dissolution. Above 150 micrograms you are getting into the heavy dose range which goes up until around 400 micrograms. Above that level, you are looking at the heroic dose, and this is where you can experience severe alterations in your perception, heavy visuals, and potential for full dissolution of the self. LSD has a longer onset than mushrooms do, so you can anticipate a longer range of experience with effects lasting anywhere from 8 to 12 hours depending on your dosage.

Finally, you have the dosages for DMT, which is the active component in Ayahuasca. The dose range for DMT, when in the presence of the MAOI that I talked about before, varies from the 10 to 70-milligram range. For your micro-dosing amount, you will be looking at the 5 to 20-milligram range. The creative dose comes in at the 20 to 40-milligram range. 40 to 70 milligrams will be your moderate dosage. Finally, the 70+ milligram range will yield your heroic dose effects. Typically, you will see these measurements converted into teaspoons or tablespoons for ease of measurement.

These are your generic dosages and as I mentioned earlier this can vary greatly from person to person. Remember the saying I mentioned before, "you can always take more, and you can never take less". Feel into these substances, especially if you are very new to them. This is something that is very important to be aware of, especially if you are doing dosages on your own. Starting at a lower threshold and moving your way up can be a powerful way to ensure you don't take too much and find yourself in a space where you're really struggling.

~ 12 ~

SET & SETTING

Now that you understand your dosages it is time to move on to your set and setting. I touched upon this topic earlier and the importance of these two factors cannot be overstated. When I talk about your "set" I am talking about our mindset. When I talk about your "setting" I am talking about your environment. Your mindset lays the groundwork for your experience. When your mental space is clouded it can cloud the medicine's ability to work with you and your intentions. I talked about your overall diet earlier in this book as well. Being aware of what's coming into your consciousness and body in the days and weeks leading up to the ceremony, especially on the day of, plays a big role in how your experience plays out. These are a few good questions to ask yourself, in the days leading up, to gain a bit of a deeper understanding of where you are at in your mind. You can go through these questions in your head or take some time and journal them to see what comes up for you:

Are there things running through my mind that will affect me?
Are there certain visuals or feelings that I am anticipating?
What expectations am I holding for the experience?
What current mood am I in?
What state of mind am I in?
What am I holding on to?
Do I have some nerves?
How do I feel?
Am I anxious or excited?

Being aware beforehand can better help prepare you and aid in your emotional stability. Also, having practices in place that can help you regulate your emotions will be important to implement at certain points in your experience. Yoga, meditation, breathwork, dance, and tai chi are just some examples of tools you can have in your toolbox to implement in your difficult times. Psychedelics manifest in the mind so the deeper of a connection and relationship you can have with your mind the better. Remember, you are never trying to fight any parts of yourself. It is all about bringing love, compassion, and understanding to all parts of your being. Through this love and compassion, you can cultivate a cohesive relationship between you and your mind. You are not your thoughts. You are not your brain. You are the conscious awareness that lies behind that. Many times, you can get caught up identifying with your mind and thoughts which leave you on autopilot. Taking back the wheel of consciousness can be a bumpy experience, especially if you have lived so many years in the ingrained patterns of your brain circuitry. This is part of the resistance that may be coming in these experiences. The brain just wants to protect us, keep us alive, and affirm our identity.

Giving up that control can feel like literal death to the logical brain. When you do allow the "death" of the brain's control you allow space for a rebirth where your true essence is once again orchestrating your experience. You gain control over life when you let go of control. Yes, this seems so paradoxical but when you experience this simple truth your life begins to shift in massive ways. Control is an aspect of the human experience that I have seen so many people grapple with within their journey. The mind wants to control, especially outcomes. All that you can control at any moment is yourself and how you are showing up to the world. Become aware of your mindset but do not judge any of it. Come in with loving awareness. This is not a fight or a battle. Do not try, just be. These are concepts that are hard to explain through language but make more and more sense as you implement these practices into your life more consistently.

Now for your setting. Where are you? Is it comfortable? Are there comforts available to you? Are there resources available? Are you in a jungle in Peru? Are you at your house? Having awareness of your setting and how it's set up is going to influence your mindset and how you feel in that space. If you are in a familiar space then you can have that feeling of being home, which can make it a little bit easier to navigate for you. If you are in an unfamiliar area where there's a lot of variables you don't know about then a lot of additional anxieties can come up. You just want to cut down the number of external anxieties that are coming in from either your mindset or your environment so that you can be fully present with the medicine and what messages are coming through for your experience.

Being aware of your set and setting will play an enormous role in how your experience plays out. I have heard firsthand stories of people taking higher dosages of these medicines while not being in the proper set and setting. This led to them not getting as much out of their experience. They experience the visuals, and their thoughts wander but other than that they failed to get the deep substance out of it. They didn't have a conducive set and setting that was providing them with a frame to have a deeper type of experience. This is especially true when taken in a more social and party type of setting where the intentions aren't necessarily aligned with that of deep inner experience. I would highly suggest not downplaying the importance of having a proper mindset and a proper setting going into your experience. Put a lot of thought and intention into this concept and you will yield experiences that can often lead to extreme breakthroughs in your consciousness.

~ 13 ~

SETTING THE CONTAINER

There is also a powerful way to open what is referred to as the "container" of your experience. A container refers to what can be envisioned as an energetic field or bubble around the space you are in. These various medicines work with our physical as well as our energetic bodies. They also have what I would describe as spirits connected with the medicine and connected with the experience. From my experience, it is a powerful practice to have a ritual that you partake in as you begin your session.

So, what do I mean by ritual? I don't mean it has to be something religious in nature. What I mean about a ritual is something for you that sets the container and intentionally opens the experience. It is opening the space and your consciousness to allow you to begin to commune with the medicine and commune with their spirits or essence. It is an opportunity for you to give thanks to the medicine, to your ancestors, to your guides, to the earth elements, and to whatever else you may feel called to really connect with and invite into the space. The more you offer your consciousness and take time to give gratitude, the more you can call in the non-physical elements that can offer you protection and guidance. When you put the intention out there you allow yourself to connect with these things that exist out of your physical reality. This process can involve music, singing bowls, chanting, or you can do prayers. It can be in a myriad of different ways and each way has its own effect and its own profound ability to really set the container and open the space up for you. Again, this is whatever looks and feels right to you. There is no certain framework or outline that says you must do it a certain way, but it's always powerful to recognize what other people are doing and to be curious about the rituals of other people. This is especially true when it comes to indigenous cultures that have been working with these medicines and spirits for thousands of years. It can be very beneficial to do your due diligence and see how they open the space and to see if what they do brings you to a deeper truth of what you wish to be doing for yourself.

This process can also be a powerful way to clear the energy of the space and to help ground you prior to the experience. Using scents like Sage and Palo Santo are very well known for clearing the energy of a given space. When going into a ceremony where you will be sensitive to energy, you are going to want to have any lingering or stagnant energies cleared out beforehand. Even though you can't see them, these energies exist within the space and can interact with your experience. Ritualizing the experience can be powerful to more deeply commune with this medicine, with spirit, with your ancestors, and allow for anything that may want to come through and be there with you as you move through this experience. Again, this doesn't have to be a religious practice, but it can be also. It's just about creating a connection to the divine, a connection to yourself, and a connection to the intention that you are going in with.

~ 14 ~

FACILITATION

So, I have talked a few times about having a facilitator or a guide for your experience. It is always going to be advised to have an experienced facilitator or a guide to facilitate the journey, especially if you don't have a ton of experience in the plant medicine space. If it's your first time it may be risky to just get a cabin in the woods and do it yourself without having someone there for support. The one thing you can expect from any psychedelic is you never know what to expect, no matter how much experience you have. I have definitely had some powerful experiences where I took higher dosages of a psychedelic alone at my house. They were very profound for me, and I felt an inner calling to sit with the medicine by myself. With that being said, I did always have someone that knew what I was doing and was readily available should I have needed support at any time. But those experiences were much further along in my psychedelic journey and after I had a good deal of experience in the space.

It's advised to always have that facilitator or guide but it's not a hundred percent necessary. You know what is best for you and you can follow that inner intelligence while still having safety precautions in place. Have someone readily available, whether it be on the phone or zoom, who understands what you're doing that night and can be readily available. There are also applications on your phone that provide psychedelic support as well. There are text and call hotlines for people that are going through difficult experiences that are available at all hours of the night. You can text and call them for support either before, during, or after your experience.

Typically, a sitter may be on a low dose or no dose at all, especially in a clinical setting. You certainly do not want your facilitator taking higher doses of the medicine as they are no longer a facilitator and they become another participant in the journey. The low dose for the facilitator is to allow them to connect with the medicine and more deeply with you and your experience. There are varying ideologies about this so just understand that you may see either come up if you are going to some sort of ceremonial event. Again, you should use caution if it appears that the ones that are supposed to be holding space are having deep experiences themselves and not exactly holding the container for others. This can potentially cause confusion, distraction, and fear in the participants of the ceremony.

The ultimate role of a facilitator is to allow you to go through your experience while providing comfort and support as needed. There is this balance that they are looking to have between being an inactive sitter and an overactive guide. An inactive sitter may just sit there and not really pay much attention to the participants and the space. They may be messing around on their phone, which isn't recommended having in the space unless for an emergency. As events are unfolding the inactive guide is offering no support, guidance, or holding of space that could prove very beneficial. On the other side of the spectrum, an overactive guide may try to talk to the participants excessively. They will be telling you what to do, what's coming next, and they may try to make meaning of your experiences. The facilitators can help guide the energies in the room (typically with music, sound, mantras) but they should allow the participants to be in the driver's seat of their experience. As mentioned, every person has an inner healing intelligence that knows how to move through the journey. What the facilitator is ultimately aiming to do is find that balance where the participant feels held but not pulled in any sort of direction.

I have mentioned the concept of inner healing intelligence a couple of times in this book so far. This is something that the organization MAPS (Multidisciplinary Association of Psychedelic Studies) and many psychedelic guide handbooks will refer to. It is a concept that you can envision like when you get a cut on your body. When you get a cut on your body you don't have to tell it how to heal. You don't have to tell your body what to do to make that part of you whole again. You can put some water and anti-bacterial on it. You can put a band-aid on it to facilitate the healing, but at the end of the day, your body knows exactly what to do and how to do it. This is the same effect that happens with psychoactive medicines and your psyche. We find that the brain innately knows how to heal in miraculous ways. That knowing is always within us and we just have to allow that process to happen. The guide may need to be there to facilitate some difficulties that come up with some resistances and there are ways to help navigate those events. At the end of the day though, they're not doing it for you. You are always doing it for yourself. It is the participant that understands their own healing.

The facilitator is not there to tell you what to be doing, to make decisions for you, to make meaning of your experience, to distract you from your experience, or to coach you. This is especially true if you have someone that's a therapist or a coach there to facilitate the experience. They need to take that coach hat off during your process and allow it to unfold. By all means, afterward, they can help you unpack your experience, and they can do some coaching with you. Towards the end of the journey, the experience may turn a bit more outward, and talking through situations can prove to be extremely beneficial and healing for you. During the experience, however, it is important for them to allow you to go through the experience and for you to make the meaning for yourself. It is between you and your spirit to make the necessary connections because this is what this work is for. This is what the medicine's doing within you. It is guiding you to your own innate healing abilities that we all have within. The number one rule under any condition is that the facilitator honors and respects the person having the experience.

There can be this tendency to want to overpower with knowledge, wisdom, and insight. The guide just must let go of all that knowledge regarding the experiences that the person is having and just be with them, listen, and observe. Doing so brings the facilitator and participants back into a cohesive relationship where they are paying full attention to them and allowing them to just express and communicate whatever it is they need to. They just allow them to be without putting them down or having any sort of judgment towards the experience. Even if they don't understand what's happening, it is alright. The participant may be reliving a trauma that they can't comprehend but the facilitator can serve as an anchor, a resting place, and a quiet center for them to lean on. It is at this moment that they don't have to solve the problems and answer the questions of the experience. They just must be in a state of full allowance. This is really such an important concept for any facilitator or guide to have a firm grasp of. A great facilitator can bring calm and grounding to difficult situations while a facilitator that doesn't exhibit these skills can bring in their own projections, instability, and lack of grounding to the participants' experience. There are experiences where having those guides can really be a make or break for the participant, especially in the beginning stages of psychedelic plant medicine use. Also, having them afterward can be extremely powerful as well. We will discuss the tools of support systems and integration coaching a little later in the book.

~ 15 ~

STAGES OF THE JOURNEY

Now, let's move on to the various stages of the psychedelic experience. Again, this is just a general outline of what may be anticipated. This can vary for different people, dosages, types of medicine, and depending on the set and setting. You may experience some of these or you may experience all of these. You start off this process with the pre-ingestion phase, where you will be going through some mental preparation. This occurs before you take the medicine. This could be the day of the experience or even in the days leading up. You may experience some physiological or some mental effects including some anxiety and nerves. You may also get some butterflies in the stomach. Just be aware that there's a potential to have some effects before you even take the medicine and that is a normal part of the process. I like to say that our process begins the moment we say yes to exploring a particular medicine. That conscious decision triggers a series of events leading up to and going past the ceremony.

Next, you go onto the ingestion portion. Here you are taking the medicine which may be some dried mushrooms, a tea, or something you smoke all depending on what it is you are deciding to journey with. After you have ingested the substance, you will then move on to the onset of effects. As I mentioned before, the different compounds all have a little bit of a different onset time and duration. For the purposes of this book, this is a general outline that is mainly focused on Ayahuasca, Psilocybin, and LSD. The onset portion of the experience is typically going to be coming in the

20-to-60-minute range. This can vary depending on the mode of ingestion as well. To give you an example, psilocybin mushrooms eaten orally will typically onset between the 40-to-60-minute range. If you would take those same mushrooms and make a tea with some lemon, you will feel a much quicker and faster onset in the 20-to-40-minute range. Same compound, different method of ingestion, different onset time. During this time, it can commonly come with a little bit of nausea, some uneasiness in the body, some discomfort, some feelings of awkwardness, and also some intense feelings of energy as your sensitivity begins to increase.

You are increasing the vibration of your body during these experiences and the medicine is doing work with your energetic body. Many times, you will feel this, and it can feel intense at moments as you reach a new baseline frequency. Sometimes it can feel like you have one foot in the door of your regular consciousness and one foot in the door of this altered state of consciousness which may feel a little uncomfortable. It feels a little "different". So just be aware that in this come-up phase, which will be passing through, you can have those feelings that are coming up. They do not last forever. After you get through the onset phase you may start moving into the first bit visuals, mental wandering, and potential purging (mostly with ayahuasca). Not everyone has intense visuals. Sometimes you may get more intense visual effects than other times. That can vary depending on the substance and strain you have taken. At this point, the mind may start wandering and going off into different areas of thought and introspection. You may start to see your brain patterns and thoughts going off in different directions. This is a very normal part of the process. A lot of times this is where the healing process starts to come to the surface. As you get through the onset, first visuals, and that mind-wandering phase you will then begin to creep into the peak phase. I will keep it generic so it's going to be a wide window, but I say you can anticipate anywhere between two and five hours. During this time, you are going to be in the most intense part of your journey both visually, mentally, and emotionally.

At this point, you may or may not experience some very intense visuals with both your eyes opened and your eyes closed. With your eyes open you may see patterns overlaying on top of the things in the room and you may see energy waves coming off objects and people. Energy waves are what I would describe as translucent wave patterns that can be seen flowing throughout the room and seeming to emanate from various things in the space. If you feel compelled to close your eyes and go inward, you may get intense visuals there as well. Many people report extremely vivid colors that are constantly changing and morphing into one another in complex geometric patterns that are beautiful and indescribable. Be aware that some intense visuals, depending on your dosage, can come whether you have your eyes open, or your eyes closed. Again, there is a chance that you have a powerful experience with no visuals at all as well so don't anticipate or expect anything from one experience to another. During this phase, you can also have intense and rapidly changing emotions. You could go from laughter to anger to sadness, and it could be like a whirlpool of emotions going on within you. A lot of things may be coming to the surface for you that have been held deep within for many years.

This is the part where difficult or "bad trips" can occur. I am subscribed to the line of thinking that experiences labeled "bad trips" are just the ones where we have the most difficult things to face within us. From my experience, the difficult ones are the ones that provide you with the most healing and insights to take away. I'm not going to take away the validity from anyone's experience and say that bad trips don't exist. I would not take away that very real feeling from anyone. I do believe that many times what people perceive as a "bad trip" are just difficult experiences that are leading us to areas that we struggle facing on a very deep-rooted level. On one level you don't want to go into that thought or pain, but on another level, you know these are the things that need to come up for healing within. While you can label the experience as bad and lock it away there is also an opportunity for you to look at what the experience is trying to point you towards and see what you may have to gain from it. More times than not, the most difficult trips that I ever had were the most beneficial to me when it came to my growth and development as a person and in my spiritual journey.

At this point in the experience, you could have a desire to close your eyes and go inside. For me, it has happened where I just had this internal feeling saying to me that I just needed to close my eyes at that moment. When I proceeded to do that, it took me on this big internal journey where I had some profound realizations. I also would have some incredible visual effects associated with this as well. Just be aware that going inside and closing your eyes is something you may feel compelled to do and you do not need to resist that call. It is not bad and a lot of times it can lead to some profound realizations within your experience. It is also important to be aware that during this part of the journey there is a potential for the loss of your sense of self to occur. I talked about my first experience earlier in the book where I had that ego integration experience or that "ego death".

There is a part of your brain that controls your sense of self that can be turned on and off, like a light switch. For me, how that showed up is I forgot everything about my life. I forgot about my identity, my family, my friends, my job, and everything else that I previously identified with and held onto. It disconnected me from the sense of self that I knew my whole life and connected me with what seemed to be everything that exists. It is something that is difficult to put into words, which can be common in the psychedelic experience. The term "ineffable" describes an experience so profound that we really can't put it into language but rather we relate to the feeling. This experience has the potential to be a scary experience. If you release into the experience, consciously breathe, and remember to stay present then you will get through it. This allows you to come out on the other side stronger, with a newfound sense of self. While my experience was a challenging experience, I came out on the other side completely changed. I was armed with a completely different perspective of who I was and who I really wanted to be. Loss of the sense of self can sound intimidating. It can be challenging but can also be a very beneficial and life-changing experience when it is all said and done.

After your peak phase, you will then start to move into the comedown portion and begin to wind down in your experience. At this point, you may notice that the brain isn't racing as much. You may begin to feel some more stability and grounding at this point. Now you may also begin to feel some exhaustion begin to onset, especially physically. A lot of energy has been moving throughout the body and mind. You are exerting a lot of energy in this process with your emotions, thoughts, and body. When you are in the peak phases you can be a bit numb to the amount of energy you are putting out. Now that the effects are wearing off, you will start to feel the effects of the energy you have been putting out. You will now be slowly coming back into the normal state of consciousness. You may still feel a slightly altered state of consciousness and you may have some slight visuals but all in all you are feeling pretty much baseline. You will feel much more grounded, and you will be continually getting back from this experience until eventually you hit full baseline and you realize you are back to your typical state of consciousness. At that time, it is good to refuel and make sure you get some water in your system. Fruit is amazing at this point as well. Fruit juice or smoothie can be extremely nourishing and taste incredible. It is best to be prepared for the come-down portion beforehand. As I said, you spent a lot of energy over the past few hours. You are going to be quite exhausted so whatever you can do to save you time and effort after will be beneficial.

~ 16 ~

LETTING GO

It is common to hear the term "letting go" in reference to allowing the releasing process to take place. This is something that is difficult to define in words. What does it mean to let go? I have heard the term repeatedly and I have reminded myself to let go during my experiences time and time again. But it was never something that felt like a conscious thing I was doing. It always felt like such a natural process that took over and was beyond my conscious comprehension. The letting go process was not always easy but when it finally happened it was like opening a dam of emotion. It is not something that I could put a finger on and describe how to repeat that process for myself and others. This is something that we work through within ourselves. At its core it is the process of letting go of control, letting go of emotions, and letting go of anything we may be holding onto from our past that is affecting us in the present.

You are releasing emotions through the physical. The process is a physical manifestation of an emotional release. This is not just an adverse chemical reaction or food poisoning going on, which is one of the myths that have been perpetuated about why we have these intense purges. As I mentioned, the releasing process can take shape in many forms. You may experience a strong urge to have a bowel movement which is most certainly a form of purging as well. If you have a group setting it is strongly advised to have multiple bathrooms ready in case multiple participants experience this effect. There can be big emotional swings of going from laughing to crying as you navigate different emotional areas within you. I have seen people go from extreme crying to extreme laughing on multiple occasions. This can be common because after your release you can find yourself laughing at what you had been holding on to now that you have had such a shift in your perspective.

You can ebb and flow in between these various forms of release as you navigate your experience. You can go from crying to trembling to laughing and back again. The key is to submit to the current of the experience instead of trying to fight the current. You cannot beat the experience into submission, so it is best to release the emotions and allow yourself to go where it is taking you. You may have to get in a good round of yelling that releases pent-up emotion. Many times, this can come from deep-rooted anger, something inside of you that just wants to be heard. Yelling this bottled emotion out and putting that out into the universe can be a powerful way to release this. Don't feel like that's discouraged because it is absolutely encouraged to put that out there and to yell what you need to yell as you feel called. Again, being cognizant of who's around and what space you're in is extremely important also. This goes back to your set and setting and ensuring that if this should come up that there is a safe space to do so without infringing on others.

Now I will discuss some practices that can be beneficial to implement during your experience, especially if you are going through some difficulty letting go. First, music can be a very powerful tool that helps to guide the energy and give your mind a focal point. Typically, facilitators will utilize music that starts with lower energy and slowly ascends along with the phases of the experience. The music can then descend as you move through the peak phase and move towards the come-down portion of the experience. I have seen some incredible effects happen when certain songs are played during a ceremony. This is a powerful tool to utilize. We are energy. When we look at humans on the most basic level, we are energy waves. The sound waves of the music are working with our energetic bodies and have a profound effect, which can really help move energy through you during some of the difficult situations that may arise.

Another powerful thing about this tool is that music transcends language barriers. It is often recommended to use instrumental music so that lyrical content does not have an adverse effect on the experience but there are also tracks with vocals that work incredibly in conjunction with the medicine. Being able to move beyond language allows us to speak in a language that everyone can understand. Everyone inherently understands music and tones, whether that is on a conscious or subconscious level. This is a powerful way to interact with people during the experience, especially as a facilitator, while not using words that could be misconstrued, heard the wrong way, or misinterpreted.

There are also breathing techniques to utilize which can be extremely beneficial in difficult situations. Your breath has an extremely powerful effect on the state of your body and he science supports this. Doing certain breathing techniques allows you to go from an activated sympathetic nervous system (fight or flight mode) to an activated parasympathetic nervous system (rest and recuperate). When you are in fight or flight (known now as fight, flight, or freeze) your energy is either moving rapidly or you find yourself paralyzed, with stagnant energy locking up within you. When you are having difficult emotions, taking the time to do some slow and intentional breathing can have a massive effect on your state of being. Take the time to really feel the air that is going into your stomach and into your lungs. Many times, this practice is the key to getting through the difficulty. Just coming back to your breathing routines and having them known beforehand will be of great benefit to you.

The use of rapé is another great tool to have in your toolbox. Rapé is a tobacco nasal snuff that includes a blend of tobacco and other herbs that are sourced primarily from the Amazon. The effect of this snuff is an extremely grounding effect, and it also allows you to move through difficult feelings and emotions more quickly. It is not uncommon to come face to face with blockages where you will have difficulty letting go and releasing into the experience. There can be resistance within you. Using the rapé is something that allows you to release these emotions when you are having difficulty letting go. I have seen this used with such powerful effects during an ayahuasca ceremony. There were times when participants were hyperventilating and attempting to move through a certain emotion, but they were just not able to let go to the experience. They were holding on to something deep inside of them and during that time they will have this rapé administered to them. Within seconds, they are often able to release the emotion in whatever method of purging that decides to come up. This may be in the form of vomit (mainly with ayahuasca), a cry, a laugh, a tremble, or however that motion wants to come through. Rapé is a powerful tool that you can use to further allow these energies to move through you and allow you to let go of whatever you need to let go of.

Sometimes it could be very powerful to talk some things through during the experience. Having a facilitator there that can just walk beside you through the experience can lead to immense breakthroughs. Again, the role of the facilitator is not to coach. Sometimes just allowing the participant to speak and be heard will allow them to come to their own realizations rather than just being up in their head. It is always encouraged to stay internal for as much as possible and to leave the speaking portion to the end of the experience. Talking does have the potential to lead to distractions and avoidance so caution must be taken. You are the one that is in the driver's seat of the experience, but the recommendations are in place to help you get the most out of your journey.

Healthy punching may be another avenue of release, especially for emotions rooted in anger. Now, this does not mean you should be going around punching people, objects, and walls. You can utilize a thick pillow, or you can also utilize the ground outside. I have seen participants utilize slapping, punching, and stomping to move intense energies out of their bodies. This is another way to physically manifest your anger. You do not have to be ashamed of your anger. You don't have to push it away. This is an emotion you are feeling for a reason. Having healthy ways to move that through your body during the experience can be very powerful and allow it to get out of your system so that you can better process the event from which it came. Try not to hold any expectations as to the way you will be releasing during your experience and don't fight the emotions as they come up. This is simple but certainly not always easy.

~ 17 ~

JOURNALING & CREATIVE OUTLETS

As you move past purging and releasing, if it is part of your experience, it can be very beneficial to implement some journaling. I will honor the fact that it may not always be the easiest to journal, especially during the peak phases. You may be experiencing heavy visuals, or your mind may be racing all over the place. I would recommend having at least a paper and pencil open and available for things that come up for you. I am so grateful that I have made it a habit to always document my experience before, during, and after. I have a journal that I utilize every time I work with a medicine. I write the date, I write the dosage, and I utilize prompts and empty space to allow messages and insights to flow through me for future reflection. I started to do this because I noticed that while I was having these profound experiences, there were lessons that were not sticking beyond the experience. I believe that on a deep level we remember and are engrained with the experience that we have but there is a power in being able to reflect on the lessons that came up so they can be further implemented into daily routines and habits.

This has been an extremely powerful practice for me. It helps with the integration process to see if you're taking the things that are being shown to you and to see if you're bringing them forward in your everyday life. As I mentioned before, if you have this practice going into the experience and you're already comfortable with journaling then it's going to be like second nature to you. I have some prompt questions here for you to reflect on during the experience which can be powerful and help guide you to thinking in a certain manner during or after your experience:

How are you feeling right now?
What emotions are you feeling?
What insights are coming to you?
What have you worked through?
What is challenging you right now?
What messages want to come through you right now?

These prompts can be very powerful. I have noticed with journaling that I can really channel wisdom and knowledge from a source that is beyond the conscious mind. The process of writing forms this connection for me and many times I find myself in amazement at what is coming through me. Sometimes all it can take is this simple practice to create a divine connection to higher truth. It really is an incredible thing to experience. Be intentional with the practice and really tune into asking the medicine questions like, what wants to come through me? What can come through me? What do I need to see? This can be a powerful way to get it on paper, to get it out of your mind, and get it from the non-physical to the physical. You do not have to use prompts. Just having an empty sheet of paper may work better and allow you to flow, write, draw, and express in different ways as well. Go with whatever feels best and what will not feel like an added stress for you.

If journaling and writing sound like too much of a tall task you can also record your experience with a phone or voice recorder as well. I have done that where I just put my phone down and recorded my night's events. I put the recorder on and let it go throughout the evening. That is something you could then go back to, and you can later transcribe it if you wish. You can even send the recording to a website and have them transcribe it for you in a matter of hours. That's also a way to get it written down and you don't even have to go back and do it yourself. There is a bunch of different options to implement for you to track your experience and take it moving forward, which is going to be beneficial when you get into the integration portion.

Having creative outlets available during your journey is another great tool for you to use. If journaling is difficult and you are finding it a struggle to put your experience into words, especially the emotions, it can be easier to express in some form of a creative outlet. Having some creative mediums readily available is suggested so that you can outlet these feelings and emotions. Musically you can have a djembe drum, bongos, flutes, guitars, singing bowls, or whatever musical instrument you feel comfortable with. Music is energy and creating music is another way to move that energy for you. Explore this energetic movement and see what tones want to come through you. Having art supplies handy is another great practice.

Coloring books, easels, a dry erase board, sketchpads, colored pencils, and paints are all great to work with. There is a very therapeutic effect to working within the arts. So much emotion can be conveyed using drawing, painting, and coloring. Emotions that you can't find words for can be conveyed in an infinite number of diverse ways. You don't have to be a Picasso or a professional musician to do these things. Energy and creativity will just want to flow through you, and you will find that it could be so healing to just play this through an instrument, scribble some lines out, or do some coloring in a coloring book. Music and art are healing on so many levels so having these available during the experience, whether you use them or not, is very beneficial. I have had multiple experiences where I felt really called to just do some drawing. I really like to have coloring books because they allow me to be creative within a structure. I have a couple of "trippy" coloring books with some awesome designs in them that really work well with the psychedelic experience.

Part 3: Post-Ceremony

So far, I have covered what you need to know leading up to your psychedelic experience as well as tools and insights to utilize during your experience. Now it is time to move into the post-ceremony portion of the book. While everything in this book has extreme value regarding preparing for your upcoming journey, this next section is most important for ensuring that you take the messages from the experience and turn that into life-long change. I am extremely passionate about the integration process and have learned so much about it as I went through my own path. What I came to learn is that there is a gap between the intellectual understanding of the experience and the actual implementation and embodiment of the lessons. The psychedelic experience is not the finish line of healing rather it is the starting point. The medicines only shine a light on the areas that need the work within you. It is then on you to implement habits that support your growth and healing after you are done. I have a dear friend that imprinted the saying "life is a ceremony" into my consciousness. When you break that down it is such a profound understanding. During the ceremony you often feel more connected, more one with nature, more loving, more compassionate, and completely in tune with yourself and the universe. The thing is, is that you do not need the medicine for these things. The medicine is just showing you areas in your life where you are cutting yourself off from all of that. Living your life like you are in a ceremony every day helps to cultivate these things more deeply within yourself.

~ 18 ~

WHAT IS INTEGRATION?

Just because you have had an altered state of consciousness doesn't mean that you are going to stay there. The actual lasting change of your experience happens in the integration process. Many times, when old patterns come back you can feel even worse than you did before if the time and energy is not spent to keep these changes lasting long term. You can have an amazing experience where you have some enormous realizations and you come out of the ceremony feeling like these old habits and patterns are gone. But if you haven't done anything to change yourself, to change your way of being, and to put habits and patterns in place to make lasting change then that old pattern can and will come back. The experience you have sheds awareness on the patterns that you have been holding onto. It is what you do with that awareness that creates the space to make the changes necessary in your day-to-day actions. If you do not capitalize on this awareness then often you may even feel worse about yourself than you did before. There can be feelings of guilt and shame that come into play. This is due to having tasted that liberation only to fall back into previous conditioning. So again, the experience is just the beginning of the journey. It is just the beginning of the healing. They are opening the doors and showing you where the healing needs to be done. What you do from there is really what makes the lasting change in your life. Repeating experiences does not lead to a maintained change in consciousness, that happens through work and effort.

You cannot just keep repeating the experiences over and over to get the change you desire. That only happens through the intentional integration work with daily conscious effort and while working on yourself along with your habits and routines. This is where your power lies. There's a saying that goes, "when you pick up the phone and you get the message, hang up the phone". What this is saying is that if you're working through a certain lesson, take the time to integrate it into your life and create habits that are going to foster a change in that habit rather than just going back and sitting with the medicine over and over. If you feel called later to go back to the medicine, you can absolutely do so. There may be other things for you to work through and other things coming up for you. If you're getting the same message over and over from the medicines and you're doing this on a weekly basis then it may be time to start to look at your integration work and how you're taking this into your life and how you're integrating it moving forward. I can't stress enough the importance of the times immediately following your ceremony. These are the most pivotal points in the experience because this is really where you can either take the experiences, take the lessons, move them forward and start to create those habits to make a lasting change or fall back into old patterns. That part is up to you.

I have talked a lot about the word integration, but what does that even mean? I want to take a moment to give you my definition of what integration means to me. The word integration gets its roots in the Latin language. In Latin, the word integral means making whole. The way I see it, there are two different sides to it. First, it is bringing the various fragmented parts of yourself back into cohesion. When I talk about the fragmented parts of yourself, I am talking about the mind, body, and spirit. When you go through traumas you have things within you that you push away. You can fragment yourself in all these different areas. There are ways that the body disconnects from the emotional pains that you experience so that it does not feel the pains of the past again. When this happens, you can become numb to certain emotional states. The body has the ability to shut down and steer clear from feeling certain emotions. This is a defense mechanism that may help you avoid feeling pain in the short term but causes more pain in the long term. Integration is bringing yourself back into a state of wholeness with your emotional body so that you can truly heal from the pains you have experienced in the past. It is about feeling comfortable with who you are, how you embody yourself, and how you are showing up to the world. The first part is the integration of the self, and the second part is the integration of the lesson. As I discussed, these medicines are showing you the lessons but how are you integrating those lessons? Integration means taking those lessons and then creating habits, patterns, and relationships that allow those lessons and experiences to integrate into your life. This is the process that creates lasting changes in your consciousness and who you are as a human being.

It is taking the experience and insights from a visionary experience and bringing them into your day-to-day life for the benefit of yourself and others. While you heal yourself you are healing others as well. This is because you are going to be showing up differently to the world around you. This work is so much bigger than yourself and it's a beautiful process. It's not always easy. It can be challenging, but that's part of the work that you are doing. You are taking these experiences from the visionary medicines, healing yourself, and ultimately healing the world. One misconception that is out there is that the medicines do the work for you which is just not true. They are a key that opens a doorway within your mind that allows you to move into the healing process. You are doing the work. You are doing the work in the ceremony, and it is up to you to do the work outside of the ceremony. While these tools are sacred and powerful, they are just allowing you to step into your own power of healing. Just remember that and having that honor for the medicine and as well as yourself is going to be beneficial in your integration process. I believe this process starts the minute you decide to sit with the medicine, and it is a continual process that is never-ending. The moment that you decide to embark on a medicine journey, your brain and consciousness understand this on a deeper level. It is already starting your process of integration for you. That's why we talked about your rituals before the ceremony and having those in place because this whole process starts in the time leading up to the ceremony. After your journey, you are then turning concepts into habits which leads to a change in your stage of consciousness. If you just have the concept without making a physical change then you are not going to ground that lesson in for the lasting changes you are looking for.

~ 19 ~

AFTER CARE

Directly following your psychedelic experience, you are going to want to replenish your body. First and foremost, you will want to be replenishing the body with healthy food and water. As I talked about before, you're putting out a lot of energy and a lot of intense emotions are coming up. You may have done some dancing, somatic releasing, or playing instruments and your body really has gone through a lot. Replenishing the body is very crucial at this point. First, make sure to get water in your body and stay hydrated. It can be easy to lose track and not hydrate during your experience for extended periods of time. You may not feel the effects but there is a good chance that you have experienced some level of dehydration over the hours. Be aware of that and get some high-quality water in your system.

Fruit is a great choice of food to have around for after your experience as well. It tastes incredible to your heightened senses and can help to get a boost of healthy sugars into your body. Some of my favorites are apples, oranges, peaches, and watermelons to have on hand and ready to go. It is typical to have built up a big appetite throughout your journey and a hearty meal often hits the spot very well. What this meal looks like can vary but the important thing here is to stay away from processed, high fat, and junk foods. I always like to have some rice, soup, and a veggie broth available afterward. I find this to be a light yet fulfilling meal that reacts well with the stomach. I wouldn't jump into ordering takeout and getting pizzas delivered to the house at this point. If you do, no judgment because as I mentioned this is your decision to make. Try to really listen to your body and tune in to what the body wants and not what the mind may be craving. I think it's best to put some thought into this beforehand because after the experience you've been through so much and your brain may feel like it just got out of a blender. This may cause you to want to make something quick and easy rather than healthy. Preparing this beforehand will prepare you to make better decisions afterward and not jump into freezer foods because it was the easiest thing to do at the moment. Take this time to thank your body for being the vessel of your experience.

While the experience is fresh in your mind it is an important time to reflect on what happened. As the hours and days go by, that experience can begin to slowly fade away like a dream. You can tend to forget some of the key things that came through on some level of your consciousness. I do believe that you remember it all and that it is ingrained in you through your experience on a deeper level. I also believe that it is very important to maintain these takeaways on a conscious level so that they can be more effectively integrated into your life. In integration work, the more you reflect the more you can take these lessons moving forward and implement them. Take some time to highlight key takeaways, key feelings, key emotions, some of the most prevalent topics that came up for you. This process can also be done verbally on your phone or voice recorder as well, it doesn't have to be written down. This is most effective right after while the experience is fresh. With this reflection, you can dive deep into this later in your integration process.

After you have replenished and reflected, it is then crucial to rest your body. Many times, a psychedelic can prevent you from feeling how tired your body really is. You may feel like you can stay up all night and that your body is not sore at all. This does not mean that the body does not need rest and relaxation, which includes the mind as well. Even though you don't feel extremely tired, understand that your body does need rest. It needs replenishment. Give it that time off to really integrate the experience and integrate the energies that have been flowing through you. It is very important for your mental health and as well as your physical health. It is best to give yourself space, especially in the days following your experience, to have time to be easy with yourself and begin to fully integrate your experience.

~ 20 ~

INTEGRATION PITFALLS

I will now discuss some common integration pitfalls to look out for in your process. First, you have your ego. The ego serves as your sense of self. This is not something that should be looked down upon. I don't believe there's anything within us that we should look down upon, push away, or hate. This is your sense of identity and that is a good thing. It's nice to be your own individual person here, wouldn't you say? What the ego does is it is constantly trying to affirm your reality and solidify your beliefs. What this means is that it will constantly want to stay in your habits and patterns, especially if you have some significant traumas that deeply embed patterns within you. If you have habits and patterns that helped you get along in life or helped you at one point, even if they're not helping you right now, the ego is going to want to stay in that identity. It wants to identify with a certain way of being. As you try to change yourself, it can be scary. Death of old patterns is a scary thing to the ego, even if it's for your benefit. Therefore, I put it as one of the pitfalls of integration. I don't want to say we battle the ego because then we will make it a battle. Remember, words create reality so the way you describe it is how it will show up for you. It's not a fight against yourself rather this is a journey of integrating with your ego. This is a journey of integrating your ego with yourself and coming to an understanding that you can have a healthy sense of self while constantly redeveloping who you are. You can begin to create a cohesive relationship instead of a battle.

The next pitfall that many people fall into is a term called spiritual bypassing. This is a term coined by a Buddhist teacher and psychotherapist by the name of John Welwood. It is described here in this quote, "the tendency to use spiritual ideas and practices to sidestep or avoid facing unresolved emotional issues, psychological wounds, and unfinished developmental tasks". What this essentially means is avoidance of the inner work. You can experience these transcendent experiences, but at the end of the day, the inner work involves going into your "shadows" and leaning into the discomfort. You avoid this by being very cognizant that you are not using these medicines to transcend or just go above your traumas. You integrate your shadow by going through them, not above them. What I mean by this is allowing yourself to come face to face with these past experiences so that you can come to a place of acceptance. From my perspective, you heal by going through your pains.

You don't truly heal when you try to run away or just make like everything's fine. It is ok to acknowledge the difficulty. When you don't acknowledge these things that are within you then you are avoiding the things that want your attention the most. This can be tricky because the ego doesn't always want to go into pain. It is constantly trying to keep you safe and trying to keep you from feeling pain, so you are working against the natural process of your brain. That's why this is a conscious effort on your part. It is easy to find yourself continually chasing a certain state of consciousness. To be sustained in a certain state of consciousness you must do the inner work to get there, otherwise, you are not going to sustain it. It's like climbing Mount Everest. If you just get in a helicopter and take it to the top it is much different than taking that journey to the top. There's a different feeling of accomplishment and sustainability rather than just being put there. That is focusing on the destination instead of the journey. This goes with whatever you do. It is all about the journey and falling in love with the process. It is the understanding that the process is where it all happens. The process is where all the growth and insights come from that we take moving forward.

If you look at a sports analogy like a football team, they don't win the super bowl because they just went out and won that one game. A team wins a super bowl because they trained for however long a football team trains throughout the year. In business, someone didn't create that multimillion-dollar company overnight. That was years and years of planning, learning, and adjusting. There were so many times throughout that journey where there may have been much discouragement and a desire to quit. If they didn't fall in love with the journey, then it would have been much easier to quit along the way. The journey is what builds you. It builds your character, it builds your grit, and it builds your ability to overcome things. You are here to be on the journey and there really is no finish line except the one you put on yourself. You are moving towards a vision, and you are always on a continual path of growth, development, and learning. It's a beautiful journey. So just focus on the journey, be here in the present, and appreciate the now. That is how you can avoid the spiritual bypassing and just recognize and have compassion for whatever it is that's coming up within you. All parts of you are good. Your shadow, your light, it's all part of you and all leading to your ultimate healing.

I talked a bit about the state of consciousness vs the stage of consciousness. This is an awesome concept to understand. A state of consciousness is something that changes throughout the day. It fluctuates. We could have a sleeping consciousness, waking consciousness, meditating consciousness, and psychedelic consciousness. These states are tied into your different levels of brain waves states such as alpha, beta, and theta. You have different brainwave states that you are in for your different states of consciousness. You can have an experience of a higher state of consciousness, which can falsely have you believe that you have changed your actual stage of consciousness. When you think of the stage of consciousness you can think of it like the developmental stages through life.

When you are growing up you go through these different developmental stages. The stage of consciousness is more of a baseline of where you are at in that moment of your life. The state of consciousness is where you can have an altered state. This is where there could be a potential trap because it's easy for the ego to get stuck in a trap of avoidance, wanting to be in that altered state of consciousness. You may go into a psychedelic experience and have this incredible feeling of oneness. You may feel that you have all the answers you have ever needed. You may feel connected to God, to source, and to everything and everyone. Just because you had that altered state of consciousness doesn't mean that you're not going back after the experience into your baseline stage of consciousness.

You may experience a different state of consciousness and you may have all these insights but then you must take them back to the stage of consciousness that you are at and do the integration work with it. Then you can continue to work and develop through the stage of consciousness that you're at. Again, this is an area where the ego can get caught up and where you could get caught in that spiritual bypassing because you get this feeling that you experienced being one with everything and that you are "enlightened" now. Just be aware that there's a difference between your state and your stage. The experiences from altered states of consciousness are there to take as a lesson. From there it is on you to do the work continually through your habits, through your patterns, and to make a change in your stage of consciousness to create a new baseline for yourself.

I love this quote by Robert Augustus Masters, "When transcendence of our personal history takes precedence over intimacy with our personal history, spiritual bypassing is inevitable. To not be intimate with our past, to not be deeply and thoroughly acquainted with our conditioning and its originating factors, keeps it undigested and unintegrated and therefore very much present". What this is saying is that when we just want to transcend our history and not think about it, not be close with it, and not understand it then it's going to be very much present in our everyday life. The less present you want to be with your traumas, with your past, and with your conditioning then the more present it's going to be in your life. That is one of the keys of spiritual bypassing. Just because it's not on your mind or you don't think it's affecting you doesn't mean you have overcome it or worked through it. I love how he uses the term intimacy here. Become intimate with your shadows, become intimate with your traumas. Again, this can be difficult because the ego wants to move us away from pain. It doesn't want us to feel it. But when you face that pain, you can move into acceptance and integration of that. You turn that pain into your power. This is such a powerful process that is referred to as alchemy. I have experienced so many stories with people who have had the most difficult past imaginable. Those who have had a past that makes you wonder how they are standing here today with the amount of success that they have. I began to understand that when we turn our darkness into light, it is so much more powerful and it's a force that gets used for us and no longer against us. So don't be afraid of your pains. It may be very difficult, but when you alchemize them, they turn into your superpower. They will turn into your beacon of light and that light will help you as well as so many others along the way.

~ 21 ~

6 PILLARS OF INTEGRATION

I use a framework of integration known as the six pillars of integration which are the six areas of your life that are going to be most prevalent in your integration process. The six pillars of development are intellectual, inter-personal relationships, mind-body connection, environment, spiritual growth, and lifestyle. Intellectual development is your personal development, your schooling, reading, what you are feeding your brain on a regular basis. Inter-personal relationships are the relationships with those around you. This is your family dynamics, your friends, and the relationships that support your growth. The mind-body connection is balancing your physical and emotional health. It is understanding your diet, where your body is at physically, and really having a deep connection to it. Environmental factors involve stabilizing your living conditions, understanding your work environment, and realizing how that may be affecting you daily. Spiritual development is about cultivating a deeper meaning and purpose in life. This is not particular to a certain religion or background. Spirituality is simply your connection to the divine, to something bigger than yourself, and to the forces you may not see but you feel. Then finally your lifestyle which includes your work-life balance, your creative outlets, and how you embody who you truly wish to be.

Pillar 1: Intellectual Development

The first pillar of integration is intellectual development. Learning is something that is so pivotable in whatever it is that you are taking part in. Clearly, you are taking the time to read this book, so you are actively investing in yourself and in your learning. You are already on the right track, so congratulations! I have broken this section down into three of the biggest areas that, at the beginning of my journey, I leaned upon. These three different areas, or mediums of information, were books, podcasts, and television. Depending on what kind of learner you are, some may be more impactful and allow you to retain knowledge more easily than others. Therefore, it is beneficial to go through some trial and error of these different ways as you stay active in your learning process.

I am always blown away by the amount of information that I can receive from just one book. Depending on the book that you read, you can be getting information that has taken years of research and countless hours to compile. In the matter of a month, you will have taken on the learnings that may have cost someone most of their life to accrue. This is the power of books and the power of taking the time to learn from the experiences of others. Remember that pretty much any book you come across today will have an audiobook to accompany it. If reading is a struggle for you then you can opt into the audiobook version and dive into that at home or when you are on the road for an extended period. I even know people that will listen to the audiobook while reading the hard copy because they find they are able to retain the information at a much more efficient rate. Joining a book club is also a powerful way to hold you accountable to your progress and put you in a different frame of mind for digesting the knowledge. Personally, when I am in a book club, I tend to take more notes and learn the information more deeply. This is because I know that I am showing up to that call every week and I will need to know what I am talking about when it comes to the discussion that we are going to have. Implementing some of these techniques can greatly improve your ability to retain the knowledge of the books that you are reading so give them a try sometime!

Podcasts are something else that I get a lot of benefit from, and it is what I leaned most heavily into when I first had my awakening experience. Before I had that first transformative mushroom experience, that I discussed earlier, I did not have any truly defined spiritual beliefs. I pretty much saw the spiritual community as a bunch of "woo woo" stuff that I did not understand. Once I had that ego transformation and my first out-of-body experience, I then found myself starving for more information about what I experienced and what is really going on here. My wife turned me on to a podcast called "The Positive Head". Let me tell you, some days I would listen to upwards of 10 to 12 episodes of this podcast, just blown away at the information and perspectives that I was hearing. This allowed me to take in many different perspectives and begin to make sense of my experiences as I began to formulate my own truths and my own solid belief system. This is the power of the podcast. A great podcast gets us into the inner workings of some of the most remarkable brains in the world. People that we may never have the opportunity to talk to, suddenly have access to their way of thinking and seeing how they perceive the world. There are podcasts that focus on success and what makes successful people tick. There are podcasts on health and how some of the healthiest people in the world sustain their way of life. Taking the time to explore these different podcasts can broaden your understanding of the world and yourself. There are countless podcasts across the streaming platforms to fit into any topic that you are interested in, including psychedelic use and integration.

Finally, there is television. While cable television may not provide content that is suited to foster your growth there are other streaming services that do have content where you can learn and grow. Gaia is a popular streaming service that is a compilation of more esoteric and thought-provoking shows, movies, and documentaries. They have full series that are dedicated to plant medicines, meditation, yoga, and plenty of other subjects that will be of great benefit to you as you travel your path. YouTube is another great resource for you to find videos about various topics that can prove to be of great benefit to your process. The point of this section is to shine a light on the fact that there is a plethora of resources around you that you can lean into as you navigate your path. I will reiterate again, you are your own best guru. These resources are here only to bring you closer to your own truth that lies within you. I think that it is important to take in the knowledge and experiences from others so that we may use that information as we develop our own truth moving forward. Never take anyone's word as your own truth. Take this information in, sit with it, see how it resonates, take what sticks, and leave what doesn't.

It is also important to understand the concept of a fixed mindset versus a growth mindset for this topic. A fixed mindset is one that thinks it knows it all, isn't really interested in learning from those around them and is not looking for opportunities for growth in every moment. On the other hand, a growth mindset is always looking for opportunities to expand. A growth mindset understands that failure is only failure when you quit, and a "failure" just gives you an opportunity to learn. All your "failures" just serve as an opportunity for you to learn, grow, and do things in a different way. Many times, it is just a signal that it is time to change your course of action a little bit. Changing your mindset around failure and what it means to fail is very crucial and has the potential to turn you into a constant learner instead of getting down on yourself at every mistake. You can learn from everybody, every interaction, every experience, and everything around you can be a teacher. If you are constantly looking for the lessons then you are programming your mind to find the lessons in every experience. They exist in every pitfall, in every good experience, every bad experience, and they all have lessons to show us along the way. This doesn't have to be just pounding the books day in and day out either. This doesn't mean that you must be reading multiple books a month or listening to audiobooks every time you are in the car (although that doesn't hurt either). This growth can show up in a plethora of different ways. As I mentioned before, there's an opportunity for growth all around you in conversations with people, reflecting on past events, and meditation. I like to use the time in my car to listen to podcasts and audiobooks. The time in the car can be very valuable to do some intellectual development, especially if you find yourself spending a lot of your time commuting or sitting in traffic.

I believe that everything in this universe is neutral, and this includes social media. Now I know that there's a lot of toxicity and censorship out there in the digital world. But if you take the time to be very intentional about what you do on there and who you interact with then it can be a powerful place to grow yourself intellectually. You can grow your connections, grow your network, and ultimately grow your tribe. Every time I log into social media, I feel like I get a great benefit due to the accounts I follow, the groups that I am in, and the people that I choose to interact with. My feed is constantly being flooded with life tips, tricks, and hacks that I then go on to implement and share. You do not have to have such a negative outlook on social media. You can take steps to make it a tool for you and something that you're learning and growing from.

You can't learn anything if you think you know everything. This goes back to the fixed mindset versus the growth mindset. I have an amazing knowledge base and I am constantly studying but I feel like I always have something to learn from those around me. Whether I am in an environment where I am teaching or whether I am in an environment where I am the student. Even when you're teaching, you're learning. There are always opportunities to learn about yourself, about others, and about the world around you. So just don't think you know everything because you will be surprised at the things you can learn when you don't hold that mindset. Learning through teaching is powerful. Taking the opportunity to teach others can really empower you to learn a lot more about whatever subject you're looking to learn about.

So how can you challenge yourself moving forward? Humans strive for comfort, but that is not where growth resides. The brain wants comfort. It wants to take the path of least resistance. Your brain is a safety mechanism that wants to keep you safe and comfortable. It wants to keep you out of harm's way and keep things easy for you. The thing is that you are not just trying to survive anymore. You are trying to thrive in life now. You must go outside of your comfort zone which goes against the programming of the brain. It is going to take that little bit of motivation and a whole lot of inspiration. Therefore, it is going to take you a little bit of discipline to move beyond that program and cultivate that deeper relationship with your brain. I think it's important to get comfortable with uncomfortable action. Little things like waking up at 5:00 AM, taking cold showers, going for a long run, and any activity where you must actively resist the brains' desire to stop. These may seem like mundane tasks but when you do things that are uncomfortable you are telling your brain, "I know you don't want to do this, but we're doing this because I'm choosing to do this". This is a muscle that you are strengthening like any other muscle in the body. You can strengthen your control over these instincts of the brain through meditation and through taking these uncomfortable actions. That is how you engrain further control and further discipline over your actions and the things that you wish to be doing.

Pillar 2: Inter-Personal Relationships

Now, onto inter-personal relationships. What do the relationships around you look like? Do you have solid growth relationships in your life? For most of my life, I didn't know what that term meant or that it even existed. It wasn't until later in life that I truly began to understand what it meant to have a relationship that fostered my growth and development. I was certainly fortunate to have had great friendships growing up. I always had friends and family around me that cared about me. But it wasn't until later in life that I understood what a real growth relationship looked like. What I mean by this term is a relationship where two people truly support one another on a deep level. It's a relationship where you ask about each other's goals, inspire one another, and hold each other accountable for what they say. Often I found myself around groups of friends that didn't put thought into the future much past what bar they were going to that upcoming weekend. I say this with absolutely no judgment in my heart but the biggest thing that I found lacking was a vision for the future. There is a saying that goes, "hang around 5 successful people and you will become the 6th". This reflects the power that our circle has upon us. If you are surrounded by people that are driven, motivated, and consciously building a future then you will fall into that standard. These relationships will constantly be pulling you to that next step of yourself. Its relationships that inherently are saying, "I love you so much that I am going to hold you accountable to being the best version of yourself that you can be, and I will be here to hold space and support that in any way that I can".

What does that support system look like for you? Who's in that support system? How are your relationships with your family? Understanding your family dynamics is important. It is important to be aware if there's toxicity in there, especially when it comes to personal development. If there is a stigma or shame around your growth and personal development, then there may need to be boundaries that need to be set within your family. Just because someone's blood doesn't mean that there isn't a need to set some boundaries. I am not saying that you need to completely cut people off, label them as toxic, and never speak to them. I am just talking about being aware of the energy you may be giving away to people that may not fully comprehend the magnitude of the work that you are doing. Just because you set boundaries does not mean you should ever look down upon or judge others that you feel don't understand the process you are in. It is of great benefit to hold compassion and understanding for all people in the world. This is the concept of meeting people where they are at. When you come from a place of love and understanding then you have the potential of having a much greater impact in their lives in ways that you may not comprehend.

Are there any things that you may be holding onto from the past in your relationships? This comes up as anger, distrust, judgment, and resentment. Holding onto these emotions in your relationships, or towards certain people, is going to manifest itself in the relationship. You are going to be bringing that to the relationship. That is only going to serve to hurt you and hurt the relationship moving forward. Just because you let go of these emotions doesn't mean that you justify the other persons' actions. It doesn't mean what the person did was okay. This just means that you are releasing the energetic bond to whatever you are holding onto with them. You are saying that you don't agree with it, you don't justify it, but you are no longer going to hold onto that emotion so that it can no longer have a negative effect on you. I truly believe that people can change, I am a prime example of that. If my wife still held onto the actions of my past before I found personal development, then I wouldn't have been afforded the space to grow into who I was meant to become. With that being said, if the people in your life are still doing the same patterns and habits without signs of remorse or change then you need to set those boundaries and maintain awareness of that. You may need to release that person from your life or keep them at a different distance moving forward. Keeping that person around while holding onto that resentment is only going to be corrosive for both parties. That's always going to leak through in the relationship. It creates a foundation for the relationship that is built on sand instead of a solid foundation built on concrete.

So how can you show up different to your relationships? Because when you show up different to the world around you, the world around you tends to change. If you have relationships where must set boundaries or cut ties it doesn't have to be in a negative, "screw you" type of way. This can be done in a loving manner. You can do it while sending the message that you love yourself so much that you must protect your energy. You can't help others from an empty cup so protecting your energy is crucial to how you show up for yourself and others. If you are showing up with love and compassion and they are not reciprocating then it may be time to put that energy into relationships that are going to reciprocate that. When you release the relationships that don't serve you, you allow space for the ones that do. This was an enormous part of my journey. Once I began to release the relationships that weren't supporting my growth, wow, the universe provided me with so many more people that were aligned with what I was doing and who I wanted to become.

Pillar 3: Mind-Body Connection

Next, I will be discussing the mind-body connection. What is your relationship to your body? Do you have communication with it? I did not have communication with my body for most of my life. I dealt with a lot of self-hate and a lot of self-defeating thoughts growing up. Subsequently, my diet and what I put into my body always reflected this mindset. I would always eat the foods that made me feel like crap because it gave me that short-term fulfillment. I didn't pay any mind to this way of being and in fact, it seemed quite normal. I always had a general interest in my health and a consistent gym routine for the most part, but I never really took the time to communicate with my body and truly listen to what it had to say. Now that I have fine-tuned my diet and taken the time to detox the things that my body doesn't want, I have noticed that my body is constantly speaking to me through feelings, sensations, and thoughts. This is the body's mode of communication. This is something that can be strengthened through clean eating and regular practices.

I have a good friend of mine that taught me a practice he does every day before his morning meditation. He takes the time to check in with his body from head to toe. He scans each part of his body inside and out, just becoming aware of the different feelings and sensations. Then, he will consciously ask his body to give him a signal of a yes. He will then pause and notice where he gets a sensation or feeling within the body to signify that yes for him. After he gets a yes, he will then ask his body to give him a signal for a no. Again, he will take a pause and scan his body for any feelings or sensations that come up which will signify a no. These sensations and feelings can vary in intensity and in where they are felt from day to day. Sometimes these signals are very discreet and difficult to pick up on. This is why it is beneficial to have a practice where you actively work on this connection so that it is like second nature when you are making decisions in your life where checking in with the body would be a great idea. The body has an intuition that surpasses our logical thinking. Turning off logical thinking and tuning into that intuition can help guide you in the right direction for a given situation. It is the same as having that "gut" instinct or feeling something deep in your heart. There is a deep truth to this wisdom that can save you energy and frustration in the long run.

Do you have regular exercise practices? We now know that exercise is very beneficial to mental health. It releases a lot of powerful endorphins and chemicals within your body that deals with mood stabilization. It empowers you with this great feeling about yourself. It gives you a nice win and it can be very profound for both your physical and mental health. This doesn't have to be pounding weights at the gym or running marathons either. This can be whatever exercise this looks like for you. This could be a routine walk or jog during the day. This could be yoga, calisthenics, swimming, boxing, or whatever else gets you moving around and active. It is some sort of practice that sends the message to your body that you are caring for it and that you are consciously taking the time to improve its wellbeing. This can prove to be very beneficial in the long term.

Do you eat foods that make your body feel good or do you eat foods that make you feel sick in the hours or days following? As I was talking about before, your body knows what you want to eat but a lot of times we partake in emotional eating. I am extremely intrigued by the body's innate ability to know what's best for it. This is what has sparked my inspiration to dive deep into my relationship with food. One of the most profound experiences I have ever had was when I decided to do a 30-day juice cleanse. It was 30 days of vegetable and fruit juices with nothing else. This gave me an opportunity to detox all the foods that were keeping me in a state of craving the things that my body did not truly want. What I came to realize is that a lot of times when emotions were stirring inside of me it led to hunger that was tied to the emotion and not to a desire from the body to eat. The times when I craved pizza, or greasy foods, was a time in my life that I was going through an emotional phase or something emotional was coming up for me. Previously I would have said to myself that the pizza is going to make me feel like crap in the morning but I'm going to eat it anyway. I would have just made that trade-off. At the end of the day, I was getting that short burst of fulfillment, but my body was ultimately paying the price for it. Understand that food can be a deep bypass mechanism. Food and anything else we put in our body can absolutely act as a drug, especially when it comes to sugars and chocolates. These foods target the dopamine receptors which are the reward receptors in our brains. I just want to impart the understanding that food can be an avoidance mechanism. A good starting point can be to become aware of when you're eating, how much you are eating, how you're feeling during and after you eat. Just bringing in that awareness will allow you to start to change some of those patterns so that you may move into some healthier ones.

Regarding mindset, your beliefs and external stressors impact your genetic expression. What I mean by this is that the way you perceive the world and the stressors that you take on can impact the way your genes express themselves. These genetic expressions impact your risk for heart disease, your metabolism, your hair falling out, and various skin conditions. All these things are genetic expressions within your body. There is a common conception that many of these things are mostly or purely heredity. Heredity is something that comes from our parents' genetics and is believed to play a huge role in our genetic expression. While hereditary traits are real, it doesn't play as big of a role as we were led to believe. Your beliefs and your thoughts can play a much bigger impact than you comprehend. When you really take the time to focus on your beliefs, focus on your mindset, and create your life with vision then you can alter the way you are expressing the genetics within your body. You have the power to alter the way that diseases show up in the body and you also have the power to reverse physical ailments. I have seen some extremely powerful stories of people with a determined mindset and healthy diet overcoming things that modern medicine said they shouldn't or couldn't be able to. When the doctors all but gave up on some, a strong belief and a healthy diet were able to counteract and change that person's life forever. Control and integration of the mind are pivotal to mental and physical stability.

This also goes back to your meditation practice. A mind is a wonderful tool. It is a great servant, but a terrible master. What I'm saying here is that when you give up control of the mind and let it just wander, then it can be easy to get lost in the many pitfalls of thought, paranoia, and anxiety. You can catastrophize situations and blow them out of proportion. But when you use the mind, and you have a relationship with the mind, then you can detach from the thoughts that race through your consciousness. You then have the choice to hold onto the ones you want to and be more intentional with the process. You then have full control over your mental and physical state. When you are in full mind-body cohesion, you are in full control of how your genetics are expressed and how your body is reacting to external stimuli.

Pillar 4: Environment

Moving on to the environmental factors of your life. It is difficult to heal in an environment that hurt you. Doing this integration work where you're in an environment of people that are putting you down and where there's constant negativity can make it very difficult to heal. I'm not going to say it's impossible, but it's going to make it a bigger challenge for you. What's your home like life? Are there shared values? Do they shame you for the things that you do, whether it be for your personal development, your growth, your habits, or your hobbies? If there is shame around those things then that can influence your growth and your ability to move through the things you need to move through. Is the environment physically safe? Are you in harm of being physically abused at all? Having a safe environment is crucial in your healing process, especially if the person that's doing that harm is part of the original traumas you have experienced. This can create a lot of incongruences, especially coming out of a deep visionary experience. Are you in threat of being removed from your current living space? If there's an underlying fear of being kicked out and evicted from your space this can create a deep sense of instability within you. Humans have a basic desire and need to feel safe and stable. When we don't feel safe it is more difficult to focus on the parts of our life that deal with development and self-realization. The mind will be clouded with a need to find that stability and comfort before it continues the path of self-actualization.

Going into your work environment. Do you work in a toxic work environment? Do you work around a lot of people that just don't resonate with what you're doing and who you are? This does not mean that everyone you work with must completely understand the journey that you're on. But if you are spending your work hours with people that are stuck in very negative mindsets, this can influence your mentality and emotional well-being. We spend a lot of time at work, upwards of 40 to 80 hours a week for most people. Understanding what that environment's like and how that is affecting you can be very important to your growth. Does the job that you do align with you ethically? Are you doing a job that's unethical because it pays the bills and it's safe? Not every job that you take must be in full alignment with what you wish to be doing.

Many times, it will be necessary to work somewhere that is a stepping stone to where you are meant to be going and that is fine. Sacrificing your ethics and moral compass to work for a job, on the other hand, can have a detrimental effect on you and begin to eat at you from the inside. Begin to understand how you align with the company you work for and how it makes you feel going to that job every day. Start to become aware if you are dreading going to work every day. Become aware of how you feel coming back from work each day and if you feel completely drained, finding yourself just wanting to shut down once you get home. This is the area in which it can be difficult to be doing the things you need to be doing for yourself and you find yourself in an endless cycle of exhaustion for a job you don't truly want to be at. Spending all that energy and focusing on how much you dislike that job can take away from the personal development work that you're trying to do when you are not there. Again, your job may be a stepping stone to something more for you, it doesn't always have to be your end goal career. It is important that you don't sacrifice your ethics and your sanity along the way. Having those steppingstone jobs that align with you can be quite beneficial and necessary at times. They can be that next step until you step into that deepest purpose that you are moving towards.

What are the shared beliefs of your culture? And for this, I'm talking about the culture of your community, home, religion, and country. Take for example western society. There's been a huge stigma around psychedelics, meditation, and many eastern philosophies. There are implanted feelings of guilt, shame, and awkwardness that surround these more esoteric ways of thinking and being. Does the culture around you look down upon certain aspects of your life? Is there guilt around that? Is there shame around that? It is important to become aware of the beliefs in your culture, how that can impact your growth, how close you are with that culture, how much that culture impacts you, and how much it means to you. As I mentioned already if there is shame associated with your way of being then you can hold this belief deep inside of you. A part of you is crying out and saying that it is not proud of who you are or what you believe. When you hold shame towards yourself it is difficult to have full love and compassion for yourself because on some deeper level there is a belief that you are not supposed to be doing whatever it is that you are doing that has that shame associated with it. Being aware of those cultural beliefs can be very important to understanding where you need to go and what you need to do for your integration work.

Pillar 5: Spiritual Growth

Next, I will be going over spiritual growth. Spirituality is a hot word that gets thrown around in a lot of contexts these days. It can have different meanings to different people, and I am not here to define what spirituality means to you. As a general understanding, I see it as practices and beliefs that deepen our relationship to our souls and to the creator. It's acknowledging the non-physical aspects of existence. This could be tied to religion, but it does not have to be. Religion and spirituality aren't competing ideologies. I think that religion and spirituality can coincide together and complement one another. It doesn't have to be that you identify as a Christian so you can't believe in spirituality or the spiritual aspects of your being. As a matter of fact, I think being spiritual can deepen your relationship to whatever religion you subscribe to. There is a disconnect that has been perpetuated throughout society when it comes to this perspective. At the end of the day, spirituality is actions moving you towards something larger than yourself. It's that connection to the non-physical, to the things that you can't see, and to the divine source of creation. It is having that belief and that faith that connect you to your purpose. This is what spiritual growth is all about from my perspective and experiences.

Spirituality is moving beyond the self and identity. It is embodying an essence that is rooted in giving back to the whole and making this world a better place than before. Again, this can be with or without religious practices. Just because you're spiritual does not mean that it negates religious practices. I believe that there's truth to be found in all religions. Religions are different viewpoints or different lenses of one ultimate truth. There is a higher power that exists within the beauty we see everywhere in the physical world that connects all things. I do believe that religions have been skewed throughout the years. Certain books have been changed in certain ways to help certain governments and to serve certain agendas. I think there have been some miscommunications and misinterpretations along the way, but at the end of the day, religion is trying to connect us to the divine and show us that at the end of the day it's all love. Love for self, the earth, humans, animals, plants, and all that exists cohesively on this planet. It's all one. Again, I think all religious and spiritual beliefs are one concept just being portrayed from different perspectives, different viewpoints. When you overlay them on top of each other and you look at the deep messages, you can see the commonalities throughout. It is about finding whatever resonates with you and with your soul. Take what resonates and leave what doesn't for you. Do your research, investigate different religions, and see what feels right for you. Don't take someone else's word, rather feel into your truths, and really find what you believe to be true in your heart. That goes for anything in life. Only you can know what is best for you and that answer lies in your heart. Listen to other people, learn as much as you can, honor their beliefs, have an open mind, but at the end of the day find your own truth and listen to it at all costs.

Everybody is spiritual, they just may not actively practice it. I think we are all souls having a physical experience rather than a physical body having a spiritual experience. There is also the perspective that subscribes to the notion that our spirit or consciousness is just a by-product of brain activity. This is from a rooted belief that when the brain ceases to function so does consciousness. I honor this perspective and will not try to take that truth away from anyone. From my personal experience, consciousness and who we truly are is something that exists beyond this physical plane. There is a single, unified consciousness that comes to this incarnation to experience separation, growth, and spiritual development. From this perspective, everyone's spiritual. Everyone has a spirit. Everyone has a consciousness. So even though they may not consciously practice spirituality, they are still spiritual beings on this planet. Some practices that I discussed earlier in the book can help to deepen your spiritual growth. First and foremost, meditation is a powerful practice to gain control over the mind and tap into that purity of consciousness that you are. A meditation practice can lead to transcendental experiences which move you beyond the mind and move you into altered states of consciousness.

I talked a lot about psychedelics in this book but that is just one avenue to travel on the path of self-realization and altered states of consciousness. Many people have just as powerful of experiences through meditation and other exercises. Breathwork is another powerful tool to implement in your routine to create powerful changes in your physiology. Intentional breathing exercises have a profound effect on your nervous system. It enables you to take control over the chemicals that are being released in your brain and throughout your body. With this tool, you have the power to reverse the effects of the fight or flight response. You can alter your blood pressure, stress hormones, and serotonin levels within the body. Breathwork can also release DMT within your brain which is naturally occurring within all humans. Your body is a pharmacy, and you are always holding the medicine. Conscious breathing allows you to reach altered states of consciousness with nothing more than oxygen and focused attention. This work can have a powerful effect on your spiritual growth as well as your day-to-day mood regulation.

Deeply communing with nature is also such a powerful practice. Nature wants to speak to you and is always there to support you. Taking the time to go into nature, and not while on the phone videotaping or taking pictures, has an effect that can be measured. It's grounding for you. You can see the effects that just 20 minutes of barefoot "grounding" outside can have on your body through modern testing. This practice changes the way your molecular structure shows up in your body. Communing with nature can really deepen your relationship with yourself and with the spirits of nature. Prayers and chanting can be another great way to connect with the divine spirit as well. This is a very powerful way to speak with spirit and have a conversation with this powerful force. It is having faith and trust in the presence of the force that makes all of existence possible. Showing that faith through these different practices can be very beneficial. This is all moving toward the understanding that we're here for something bigger and greater in this life. It is the understanding that this life is not just about us. It's about all of us on this planet. It's about the interconnected web of consciousness that's going on within this world. This is tapping into the roots of what spirituality is and what religion is trying to point us towards. Helping one another and being there for one another through the craziest of times. I think spiritual growth goes hand-in-hand with personal development. As you develop yourself and you work through your triggers you are working on your spiritual growth simultaneously.

Pillar 6: Lifestyle

Finally, I am going to discuss your lifestyle. What does your work-life balance look like? Are you finding you're spending most of your energy at work? Now, if you love what you're doing, and you are fully aligned in your purpose that is great. I'm not going to tell you to work less but I will tell you to just be cognizant of why you're working so much and who may be sacrificing due to the amount you are working. Many times, a trauma response of yours can be digging into work excessively. It could be avoidant behavior of wanting to avoid certain situations or certain emotions because it's easier to just put all your energy into work rather than to face the things that may need to be faced. Just become aware of that work-life balance and how you are spending the time with the ones you love the most. You have bills to pay, you have a mission to fulfill, but just because you have that mission doesn't mean that you should be taking away from the ones that love you and potentially hurt them in the process of it all.

What are your hobbies and creative outlets? I think it's important to have hobbies that you do out of passion and not necessarily for monetary gain. This can be a conventional outlet like art or music, but also whatever expression looks or feels like to you. I have a couple of creative outlets that allow me to tap into the right side of the brain which is responsible for your creative thinking. I believe that we are all creators here and there is a healthy quality to releasing this expression throughout various mediums. You could do woodworking, singing, drawing, cooking, or whatever creative expression looks and feels like to you. These practices help you to get ideas and feelings out of you and it allows source energy to express itself through you. I truly believe you are meant to be doing that here in one way or another. So having that as part of your normal practice can be powerful for your mental health.

Lastly, how do you have fun and let loose? When was the last time you honored your inner child? Do you make time to just have fun and enjoy life? You have an inner child that lives within you that wants to experience pure fun and amusement. Often, we are led to believe that at some point we must grow up and that there is no time for childish play anymore. I believe that we only grow up when we decide to. You are here to have fun and enjoy this experience called life. The purpose is not to work hard, be stressed, and lose the wonder of all that life has to offer. There is wonder and amusement all around if we choose to embody that within us. It can be as simple as going out and playing in a rainstorm or swinging on a swing set at the park. It can be easy to lose touch with this simple beauty of life when the stresses are weighing so heavily. This pure joy and fun are always there, waiting for you to tap into at any moment of any day. I went to Disney World on my honeymoon. I tapped into my inner child for a week and just let myself feel like a kid again, enjoying the rides, shows, and amusements as if I were back in my teenage years. Disney is most likely not the number one honeymoon destination for all couples, but my wife and I wanted to celebrate our marriage by having a week of childlike enjoyment. And we did! I like to tap into that inner child and just have a silly play while not feeling guilty or weird about it. It can be easy to have shame around acting like that but just because you grow up doesn't mean you have to lose touch with that inner child, no matter what anybody says. Life can tend to grind you down if your focus is constantly on bills, responsibilities, and anxieties.

We have become such creatures of worry and anxiousness. We don't take nearly enough time to just be, to just exist while releasing these heavy burdens of the brain. It is so important to connect back to that because I believe that the purpose of life is to create meaning for ourselves. It is to just be and to learn, grow, and evolve while having fun and loving one another. This is why you are here having this experience. You have friends, music, all sorts of things to make this experience wonderful. You are here to have a good time! It is not without its struggles and difficulties but there is always a silver lining and an underlying message to be found. So just remember what it feels like to just be joyous. I know when I was in my depression, I lost sight of this concept. I didn't honor my inner child or even know he was in there. Now that I have overcome that blind spot, I know to honor that part of me. I can clearly see the detriment I was doing to myself along the way. Now I make it a point to have this be a very regular practice for me moving forward. We become the sum of our regular practices. This all plays out in your daily habits and routines.

~ 22 ~

HABITS & ROUTINES

In the last section of the book, I will be discussing ways to put together resources and routines that will enable you to effect lasting change in your life. Your daily habits, routines, and practices are where the leg work of your process is taking place. Your habits are either bringing you closer to who you wish to become or holding you back to some degree. To be able to change these patterns you must first become aware of them. Awareness is an enormous catalyst of change. If you are unaware of your actions and how they are affecting you, then it is much more difficult to change them. I have gained great benefit from implementing one very powerful exercise that shines awareness on the various areas of my life. The exercise that I am talking about is commonly called the wheel of life. This is something that I do monthly in my reflection practice. In this book, I have discussed the six pillars of integration which are six areas of your life that you can bring awareness to. This exercise is not limited to those six areas, and you can mix and match ones that you feel most called to explore in your own life. This practice is a great way of getting a great bird's eye view of where your energy is going and the level of satisfaction you have in those different areas. The more you bring awareness to the areas of your life, the more you can make those changes. The wheel of life is a circle divided up into pie slices that are then shaded in.

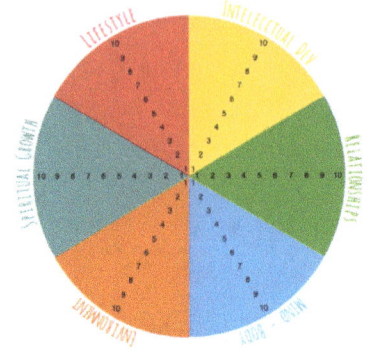

The pie slices are labeled on a scale of 1 to 10 and you shade in the area up until the level of satisfaction you feel with that area of your life. The point here is not needing to have 10's in every area all of the time. This is a snapshot of the work you are doing in your given timeframe. Many times, as you develop in one area there may be others that fall to the side a bit. For example, I may have a month where I did a lot of work in my career and spiritual growth, but my relationships not so much. This exercise then gives me the awareness that next month I'm going to focus more energy on that area. Being able to fill this out on a regular basis and see these represented puts so much power in your hands and over your life. You can always adjust these categories and add what you need to give the best view of your life along with the work that you are doing. This is something that's really going to make an enormous impact on the integration work for you moving forward.

I didn't always have daily routines that I implemented into my life. When I got serious with personal development, my daily routine is where the basics were that enabled me to change my life and allow me to become the person that I am today. The morning routine is where shifts can be made that can completely alter the trajectory of any day.

What does your typical morning routine look like for you? Do you greet the day or does the day greet you? The morning routine is an opportunity to set the day on your own terms. It can be easy to get up and get lost in the world around you before ever checking in with yourself. You get up to find yourself checking emails, social media, the news, bank accounts, and all of this allows these external factors to come flying at you first thing. All it takes is one negative factor to completely throw you off and start a snowball effect for your day. You may have heard of those days where you experience something in the morning which then cascades into a series of events that we then label a "bad day". One negative interaction has the power to affect our thoughts and emotions which will, in turn, continue to affect our mindset and decisions for the rest of the day. While this is true for negative events, the opposite is true for positive events as well. You can snowball into an incredible day when you start your day with meditation, gratitude, journaling, some time in nature, or whatever this may look like to you. The point of this morning routine is taking the time to get centered with yourself before the external world comes flying at you. We are bombarded with information coming at us from every angle throughout the day. Think of this morning routine as a way to create a shield around you so that these external factors can't immediately have an effect on your emotional state. You are continually building an armor around yourself that enables you to show up with more resilience to all the things that life has to throw at you on any given day.

The amount of time spent during this morning routine is up to you and can vary from day to day. You can have a routine that you complete in 20 minutes and ones that take a couple of hours depending on what you feel is needed for you at that moment. It is whatever you need to wake up and really get into a positive state of mind to get ready for the day ahead. This has played such an enormous role in my growth, and I know it can be in yours as well. Mine has evolved and changed over time also. I found that it is important to have flexibility in the routine so that it is sustainable in the long term. The morning routine is not a list of things that you "must do". I look it at as a set of practices that you choose to do because you know that they ultimately lead you to feel better and start your day with the best mindset possible. As you explore this routine start to take note of what practices make you feel the best and make the most impact on you. This can begin to develop your list of "non-negotiables". These are the things that you realize would greatly benefit you if done on a daily basis. Having those non-negotiables will enable you to create the most impactful routine to stick to on a consistent basis. If you don't already have some sort of routine, you can start small with one or two things for a couple of minutes to get you going. See how it makes you feel and see the things that you find most important to start your day with. From there you can begin to adjust and add more practices to it slowly. I have found that trying to dive into an enormous change can often lead to an eventual burnout and reverting to before. It is the small incremental steps that empower you to create sustainable change in your life. Now when difficulty arises in your life you will find that you can handle them in different ways than before. You will have a newfound clarity that will enable you to make decisions that are most aligned with where you wish to be going.

Planning is another powerful aspect of the personal development process. How are you planning your days, weeks, months, and years? When I started to implement a daily and monthly planner into my life things started to shift in very big ways. I understand that not everyone is the same and that not everyone feels called to plan things out, especially in some sort of a planner. I also have come to understand that there's enormous power in setting goals and tracking where your time and energy are going. I find that there is this balance that can be achieved between structure and flow. I have my military background along with a very left-brained (logical) way of seeing things, so I love structure. What I realized through my journey is that having too much structure can be a bad thing as well. We have a certain balance of structure and flow that works best for us and that varies depending on individual personality, beliefs, and how we best function. What works for one person will not necessarily work for another, so this is where it is important to deploy self-awareness of what is effective and ineffective in your life. I have a weekly planner where I can create a framework for my week. Instead of having every day filled out from start to finish, I utilize the planner to create goals for each day. I will fill in the things that must happen at certain times throughout the week and then leave space for me to have flexibility throughout the days. Some weeks I find myself having much more structure, especially if I have some deadlines that I am aiming to hit on certain projects that I am working on. Other weeks I may just have a few things filled in and I allow myself to have a more plug-and-play type of schedule. I plug and play with the goals that I have set forth for that week. That is the key part of my forward momentum. Every week I make a list of the goals I aim to achieve, and I have them listed in order of importance. This list is my go-to when I find myself wondering where to put my energy at any given moment.

For setting those goals I use a framework that is known as SMART goals. This is a way to set up goals so that you're better able to achieve them. The acronym stands for specific, measurable, attainable, realistic, and time-bound.

Specific – Making sure that your goals are not too broad. The more specific you are with your goals the easier it is to begin to take your action steps. This also makes it easier to form an emotional attachment to the goal at hand.

Measurable – This is to ensure that you will be able to track your progress and to know you have attained the goal that you set out to do.

Actionable – It is important to ensure that your goals are reliant upon your actions and not the actions of others.

Realistic – Being honest with the capabilities of achieving that goal. This is not meant to make you play small rather it is to help ensure that big goals are broken down into smaller ones and that you are employing awareness around the goals you are setting out to attain

Time-Bound – Putting a time frame on goals prevents them from being goals that continue to be pushed further and further along. Setting a time frame creates urgency and tells yourself when you wish to have this accomplished.

There is one other key factor that can make you unstoppable at achieving your goals. This last factor is the emotional attachment, also known as your "why". Answering the question of why you want to do something is pivotal in any decision that you make in life. With a strong why there is no barrier that cannot be overcome. People that achieve some of the most incredible feats of all mankind have tapped into a deep reason for why they do what they do. I have found that having a why which is rooted in something internal is much more sustainable than those rooted in the external. When a reason for goal achievement is rooted in purpose, love, serving something greater than yourself, or making an impact in the world then you can move mountains. When the reasons are rooted in the achievement of material things, chasing other people's dreams, or in something that doesn't deeply emotionally involve you then it's much easier to give up when the inevitability of difficulty and struggle comes up. When you are firm on your why, the how will show up. The logical mind loves to define the how and when you don't clearly see the how then your mind will try to find the reasons why it should not move forward. You override this mechanism by developing that deep sense of knowing as to why you must move forward with what you want to be moving forward with. This is your super-power. This is how you can achieve anything you truly desire without having to have had the "how" of it all figured out. The how will present itself and usually in ways that go beyond the logical, thinking mind. When we try to beat our life into submission with logic, we often close doors of opportunity that are waiting for us at every turn.

This visual planning process also serves another powerful purpose. When you track your days and weeks you are applying another layer of awareness on your habits, routines, and how you spend your days. I mentioned earlier that I don't have every minute of every day planned out, but I do aim to completely fill out where I spent my time every day. I will either do this continually as my day moves on or I will take time at the end of my day to reflect and fill in how my day was spent. This allows me to take an honest look at how I was spending time throughout my day. From that awareness, I was then able to adjust, shift, and ultimately find more time in my weeks that I previously didn't understand I had. This is not meant to bring shame or guilt in any way. Just because you spent a particular amount of time watching television or taking afternoon naps does not mean you should look down on yourself in any way. This is only meant as a way for you to see where that time is going so that you begin to implement the most effective strategies for your days. Many times, it can feel like there are not enough hours in a day to get what we wish to get done. This is an opportunity to find those hours. I was able to find massive amounts of hours throughout my weeks by simply laying awareness of where my time was going. There were dozens of hours in my week that I was able to take back control over and implement in more effective ways.

When I began to be honest to myself about my time than I really started to open enormous amounts of space in the various areas of my life. I became hyper accountable to myself and to my vision of my life. Again, I understand not everyone reading this is going to feel called to track everything in their life and utilize a planner. That is just fine, and I am not here to say that this is the only path to making your days most effective. This is what has worked for me and can look certainly look different for you. The important part is putting thought into the goals of your days, weeks, months, and years. Setting goals is a type of visualization for what you want to achieve in your life. It helps you to move towards the ultimate vision you have for yourself. If you struggle holding yourself accountable, have someone in your life that can help hold you accountable to these goals. This is where having family, a coach, a therapist, and those growth relationships can be so pivotal.

Journaling is another tool that I utilize regularly to help me maintain awareness over my physical, mental, and emotional states. This is something that has been discussed in both the pre-ceremony and during-ceremony portions of the book as well. Looking at the habits of self-made successful people, you will see that journaling is a powerful tool for the toolbox. It is an opportunity to get out of your head and to get your thoughts and ideas into the physical. It can be easy to be get caught up in the forward momentum while not taking time to check in with yourself. Journaling is a time to connect with how you are feeling, the thoughts in your head, and whatever else may want to be expressed through you.

This can also be done with a recorder or on a voice note as well if you have a resistance to the written journaling process. There is no certain type of way that this must look nor is there any certain type of thing that you are supposed to be journaling about. Going back to that inner healing intelligence, when you put the intention of reflection into your life you will write or record what needs to come through at that moment. You can use daily prompts or an empty sheet of paper. I find myself utilizing both of those ways depending on how I feel at that moment. The point of this exercise is just to bring awareness to your feelings, your progress, and your days. It can prevent you from going through the days and weeks without ever looking back on the actions you are taking and how they are making you feel. I feel that without this practice it is easier to get stuck in patterns that hold you back for much longer periods of time. Also, this practice helps you to honor the progress you are making daily. Honoring your progress and really feeling it sets off a chain reaction of reward chemicals in the brain that will keep you motivated and driven to keep achieving more goals. It has a cascading effect that helps you in the long run.

I study a lot about personal development and listen to a lot of public speakers. If there's one common thread between all of them it's a gratitude practice. Practicing gratitude for what you have now and cultivating gratitude for the things you have coming to you.

Deep happiness can come through immense gratitude. There are countless people on this planet that would do anything to be in your position for one reason or another. That could be financially, emotionally, or physically. It can be so easy, especially with social media, to focus on what we don't have and admire those that appear to have more than us. When you turn that lens the other way around to people that have less than you, then you are able to generate a different feeling within. You generate gratitude for what you have and an appreciation for the fact that a lot of people wish they had what you have in some way, shape, or form. This makes it easier for you to generate unwavering internal happiness while also calling even greater things into your life.

If you are not grateful for what you have you are not calling in more of what you want. You are inherently telling the universe that you are not appreciative of what you have so that creates a blockage for bringing in more of what you desire. I enjoy doing my gratitude practice first thing in the morning along with my journaling. I take time to write down what I am grateful for that day and then take a moment to really feel the feeling of it. It is a 2-part process which is the intellectual knowing and the emotional feeling. Next time you practice gratitude, lay awareness on the feeling that you can generate for the things in your life you are grateful for. I know that there may be situations occurring in your life that may make it hard to find things to be grateful for and for this I just suggest you start at the basics. Your health, food on the table, a roof over your head, the earth, family, and anything else that you are blessed to have on any given day. Starting here will begin to bring more into your life to be grateful for, piece by piece.

Meditation is another cornerstone practice that will enable you to see a sustained change in your life. This is another topic that I discussed a couple of times in this book. This is you cultivating that deeper relationship with your mind. It is not trying to shut the brain off. It is not telling it to shut up, so you just sit there with a blank brain the whole time. Meditation is about becoming disconnected from your thoughts and becoming the awareness behind the thoughts. It is about watching the thoughts float by and not allowing them to take hold of your consciousness. The process of meditation is aimed at developing a deeper relationship with your brain, rather than allowing the brain to take control over your consciousness and over your life at times. It does not have to be viewed as a power struggle and you shouldn't view the brain as the enemy. The brain is a part of you and a very powerful part of you at that. If you try to fight the natural tendencies of the brain, then you will find yourself in a constant power struggle with it. That is why I use the term of cultivating a relationship with the brain. Although there are parts of you that don't always work most effectively, this does not mean that it has bad intentions. Remember that I discussed the brain wanting to always keep us safe and to affirm our beliefs. Going through any type of change or unknown is a potential threat that the brain may want to prevent you from experiencing. The more you try to fight and override this tendency the more pushback you can experience in your life. To love yourself you must love all parts that make you up. Meditation is bringing love to these parts and just observing them as they come up.

There are many different types of meditations and I suggest you explore different types to see which are most impactful for you. You can do guided meditation experiences that take you along a particular mental journey. You can do meditations that have particular frequencies played which interact with the frequency of your body in certain ways. You can do silent meditations where it is just you and your thoughts in a quiet container. You can take part in group meditations that bring the power of the collective together for transformative experiences. None of these are better or worse, they are just different and serve certain purposes. I do not stick to one particular type of meditation, and this is something that I do intuitively each time I go into my practice. I find a benefit from all the various modalities and choose not to exclude the use of any type. Begin to explore what your definition of meditation is and in what ways you are getting the greatest benefit from the practice. Also, this does not have to be hours a day you are meditating either. Some days I meditate for much longer periods of time while others I find I am called to sit for a shorter period. It is about the result you receive more than it is about the amount of time you spend in your practice. If you are getting the benefits and the connection that you are seeking then that is what you can focus on. There is no need to compare with anyone else's practice or feel bad that you are not spending hours a day in meditation. These practices are for you and only you know what feels and works best for you.

A nighttime routine is also a great practice that helps set you up for the following day. This is the time to wind down from the day and create a clean slate moving into the sleep state. When you don't take the time to wind down then you can bring the day's energies into your sleep and eventually into your next day. A lack of preparation before bed can lead to altered sleeping patterns, difficulty falling asleep, and difficulty remaining in deep levels of sleep state. You may be consciously asleep, but your brain is running as if it were awake. As a matter of fact, the brain does not know the difference between the sleeping or waking states. The experiences in the dream state are just as real to the brain as the experiences in the waking state. So, if the brain is clogged up with stresses and worries going into sleep then this will play out in the dream space one way or another. Your circadian rhythm is your body's natural process of going to bed and waking up. This rhythm is due in large part to the external factors being taken in by the body. If directly before bed you are spending a lot of time on electronic screens, then you can begin to mess with that circadian rhythm. There is a certain frequency of light emitted off these electronics that signal the brain that it is not time to go to bed yet. This results in a drop-off of your body creating a chemical called melatonin.

Melatonin plays a crucial role in your ability to fall asleep along with other sleeping functions. Melatonin is also a very common over-the-counter product that many people who struggle falling asleep take. If you are doing things that are signaling the body not to produce melatonin and then supplementing with external melatonin then you are actively creating a feedback loop that creates a dependence on the external source. I am not against using external supplements to help in times of need. I honor that there are circumstances where an external supplement is beneficial and sometimes needed. I think it is always important to explore the reasoning behind the supplements you choose to take and see if there are ways in which they can supplement from within. I utilize a concept known as the 3, 2, 1 rule that I find very beneficial. The concept is simple:

3 - Don't eat three hours before bed.
2 - Don't engage in heavy mental work two hours before bed.
1- Don't be on electronic devices one hour before bed.

When I began to implement this schedule into my nighttime routine, I began to see a big shift in the quantity and quality of my sleep. This eventually translated into how I was starting my days as well. The better of a mental state you go to bed with the better of a mental state you will wake up within the morning. There is a correlation between the two, so preparing for your day starts before the day even starts. This time at night is a great time to reflect on the day in your own way as well as plan for the day ahead. I found that this planning has greatly reduced the amount of time I spent in my bed while staring at the ceiling and wishing I could fall asleep. I have definitely been guilty of going to lay down to bed at a certain time only to find myself still laying there hours later with endless streams of thought bouncing around in my head. I did this to the point of exhaustion at multiple points in my life and it was extremely draining for me. My anxieties would really take hold and not let go. The antidote to those anxieties is action and planning. Your anxiety feeds off the unknown and off worry. The more you can fill in the blanks and put action into the place the more you can keep the anxious mind from manifesting itself.

Just like with everything else, begin to explore different habits. Try on different ones and see which ones work best for you. The best way to know what is working for you is to become actively aware of how you feel and how the things in your life are going. Become aware of the amount of ease or resistance you are feeling. Become aware of your baseline emotional states and when you find yourself more agitated or out of control of your emotions. These are all guideposts that are there for your investigation. Your emotions are a tool to help you find the places within you that are seeking healing. When you come to your circumstances with curiosity you find that all the things you experience are with purpose and are guiding you if you look closely. I cannot press upon the importance of daily routines enough. This is where the change occurs over time. This is the essence of the integration work. This is where you create habits, and those habits create lasting change in your consciousness. It changes who you are and how you show up from the core. Take a serious look at your daily routines and develop the ones that work for you, that resonate with you, and take them moving forward so that you can become the person that you truly want to be.

~ 23 ~

SELF TALK

The final piece I will talk about in this book is your self-talk. Your conversation with yourself is the most important conversation you're going to have all day, every day. Your outer world is merely a reflection of your inner world. What do I mean by that? I mean that you literally speak your reality into existence through your beliefs and your self-talk. If you believe money is hard to come by, if you believe that all relationships are difficult, and if you believe that all people are liars and cheaters then those are all things you are going to be calling into your life. I mentioned before, your brain serves to affirm your reality and belief systems. A great example of this is when you go to buy a new car. What happens when you have a particular car that you really want? You start to see that car everywhere! You are focused on that in your thoughts and then you start seeing that car everywhere. That is the power of the subconscious mind and how it manifests your desires in physical reality. The subconscious does not label things as good or bad it just brings in that which you focus your attention on. That is why it can be ineffective to focus on not doing something. If you focus on not smoking you are still focusing on and giving power to the act of smoking. The power comes in focusing on what you do want rather than focusing on what you do not want.

    This goes with everything in your life and with the way you see the world. If you see the world as a scary and fearful place, then that is how it's going to show up. Now I am not saying that you should not honor the very real atrocities and pain that is experienced upon this planet. This is not about living in la-la land while ignoring the real things going on around. There is a difference between ignorance and choosing not to allow fear-based emotions into the consciousness that will steer the decision-making process. If you continually tell yourself that the world is a scary and dangerous place, you are going to constantly bring things to your experience that are going to affirm that belief, the same way your brain brought that car in. You can honor the fact that there are challenges going on while also honoring the fact that we are currently breeding a new age of existence into reality right now. You can see this as a time for immense opportunity to change the ways of being that have not been working for so many years upon this planet. Right now is a time where humanity is coming together to build a brighter future based on love and respect for one another and the planet. Not everyone is in line with that vision but there are too many people aligned with it for there to be any other outcome. We are moving past a time of oppression, greed, and hate to move into a golden age of love, compassion, and abundance.

That's the reality that I am choosing to call in right now. In turn, these are the experiences that I'm calling into my consciousness on a regular basis. Now, this doesn't mean that every experience I have is positive and that my life is sunshine and rainbows all the time. However, this does mean that I keep my eye on that vision and I don't allow the difficulties to bring me into a mental state of anguish. It deepens my resilience and reminds me that although there is pain, it is all for a greater purpose and ultimately serves my highest good. It is these small reframes that make an enormous impact on your life.

The following are some of the most powerful and common reframes that I have come across and implemented in my life. Going from:

> "I'm a failure" to "I'm learning"
> "I can't do that" to "how can I do that?"

"I can't afford that" to "how can I afford that?"
"I'm trying to do something" to "I am doing something"
"I am not a morning person" to "I am learning to enjoy mornings"

The most powerful words you speak in your life happen after the words I am. "I am" is the most powerful statement that you can make at any time. When you claim "I am" you are stating that this is your way of being and you are affirming that to yourself and the universe. You always have the capability to change those claims at any point. You can choose not to as well and that is absolutely fine, but it is important to understand that the choice is in your hands. This does not mean that the process is necessarily easy or happens overnight. Deep layers of programming, conditioning, or addiction can play a big role in this process as well. The brain's desire to stay the same is also another factor that may be working against you. So don't give your brain more ammunition by affirming to it a certain identity, especially if it doesn't align with who you wish to become.

These simple reframes are going to begin to get your mind working in new and exciting ways. Taking for example when you say, "I can't do that". That is a closed-loop for the brain. It is saying that there is something to do, you cannot do it, therefore the brain does not need to put any more energy into that activity. By simply rephrasing to "how can I do that?", you are now creating an open loop of thought in the brain. Now the brain is going to be looking for solutions rather than accepting the fact that you cannot do a certain activity. This is an example of how you place limits on yourself when in reality you are limitless. You have every right to not want to do something so there is nothing wrong with saying you can't do something and leaving it at that. It is very valid, but again I am bringing this point up to show you the power you have to take control over every aspect of yourself if you should choose to do so. Human beings are not meant to be compartmentalized or placed in personality boxes. We are fluid and ever-changing like everything else in the universe. You only become something static when you hold onto a certain identity or way of being. Just know that you can shift and move in and out of these various identities as you grow, develop, and evolve. To embody the version of you that you are striving to become it is important to release the parts of you that no longer serve you. The parts of you that you no longer identify with.

These simple reframes literally change the way your brain and your thought patterns operate. This can lead to immense changes in your life in ways that are difficult to comprehend. Become cognizant of your mental talk and of the mental talk of those around you. Understand that it has a very real impact on how your brain is going to start to look for solutions or start to look for problems in your life. There is a powerful exercise that you can do to begin to understand the programs or "stories" that are in your belief systems. This exercise is commonly referred to as "old stories/new stories".

On a piece of paper, write down some of the stories that play in your head which hold you back to some degree and that don't allow you to step into that newer and more empowered version of yourself. These stories can look like this:

> *"I am not good enough"*
> *"I am not worthy"*
> *"Life is too hard"*
> *"I deserve to be alone"*
> *"I am not special"*

You may not be consciously saying these things to yourself, but these core beliefs can dictate a lot of the actions that you take. At the root of your blockages is some sort of belief system that has been molded throughout your life for a myriad of reasons. These beliefs are typically put in place as a defense mechanism that is aimed at preventing you from feeling a certain pain or emotion from the past. Again, this is not for you to feel bad or judge yourself in the process. Just have a gentle curiosity as you explore these beliefs and how you can begin to reshape them to work for you. On the same piece of paper or on a separate piece of paper write your new stories that will take the place of these old stories that no longer serve you. It is helpful to do it on a new piece of paper because then you can take the old stories and safely burn them. Burning the paper with your old stories symbolizes a burning of the bond you have with that story. It does not mean that those stories are suddenly gone and will never show their face again.

It will take your daily conscious effort along with your routines to ground your new stories into your consciousness. This is another exercise that you can benefit from doing on a regular basis like the wheel of life. Whether it's weekly, monthly, semi-annually, or annually it is up to you. You will not regret taking the time to explore the stories in your life so that you can make some that will empower you to live your absolute best life. Your self-talk is a conversation with yourself and a conversation with the universe. It's some of the most important conversations you're going to have in your life. You create your reality. You speak it into existence, through your thoughts, emotions, and self-talk.

~ 24 ~

FINAL WORDS

Integration is a continual process. I believe that if we are on this planet we are growing and learning. Our learning is a never-ending process of evolution. Until the day I take my last breath I will still be learning, integrating, and going through this process. I don't think that integration is something we have a finish line for. Things are always changing in your life. Your relationships around you are changing. Your environment's changing. The world is changing. This constant state of flux leads to us always going to have things to continue to integrate and to continue to work towards. I just want you to have this perspective of understanding that the integration process begins the minute you bring your intention to change, it continues into the visionary experience, and eventually on through into your everyday life.

Fall in love with the process. Fall in love with the journey. This is amazing work to be a part of. This is the leading edge of where the new world is being built from. A lot of people are asleep to this kind of work. I know that I sure was for most of my life before understanding there was a more effective way to go about life. So many people don't have a grasp on the power of personal development, and you are at the forefront of an amazing movement. You are one of the few percent of people doing this work and taking an active part in your integration. So, honor and congratulate yourself on that. You're doing amazing work and although it can be very difficult at times it is always rewarding in the end.

Once again, thank you. Thank you for investing your time and your energy into yourself, your personal development, and your integration process. I also want to thank you for investing your time into energy into my resources. I love nothing more than taking my personal experiences along with all the things that I've learned along the way and putting them into resources that facilitate the healing and growth in those around me.

I've left a few links on this last page for some further resources that you may find beneficial. First, join our psychedelic integration community on Facebook! I am an administrator of an awesome Facebook group that is specifically geared towards psychedelic integration. We share stories, we schedule movie nights, we do group calls, and we lean on one another through our processes. We also constantly provide tips, tricks, and resources that are all aimed at helping you in the integration process and we would love to see you in there!

I also have a link in here to book a free integration call with me. If you have gone through this book, you have shown me that you take your integration and your personal development seriously. I want to offer you the opportunity to hop on a one-hour phone call where we can talk about this book, talk about the things you got from it, and how are you going to start implementing these lessons moving forward. This is also a great opportunity for me to learn what was most impactful about this book and what I could do differently in the future. My ultimate vision is to make the biggest impact on the most amount of people that I can. The more I can learn about your experiences, the more I can learn about what I did right, what I may be able to do better, and how I can better serve people in the future. That means so very much to me. This is also a great opportunity for us to discuss if you would like to explore what a psychedelic coaching relationship would look like. This is something that can be implemented leading up to psychedelic experiences and then coaching outside of the psychedelic experiences afterward to help in the integration process.

Integration coaching is something that I'm deeply passionate about as well. It is something that I know would have been so crucial when I was going through my integration work. I am constantly aiming to develop and offer the resources that I know would have been beneficial to me as I navigated my journey of psychedelic use and integration. I would love to discuss more what that looks like, what that means, and how us working together can be beneficial for both of us. Again, thank you so much for going through this book and for taking this time out of your busy life. I really look forward to seeing you in the group and to connecting with you on your free integration call!

Scheduling Link

https://calendly.com/thepositiveveteran/integration-call-book

Facebook Group Link

https://www.facebook.com/groups/299320451964168

~ 25 ~

REFERENCES

- Haden, Mark. *Manual for Psychedelic Guides.* Mark Haden, 2020.
- Buller, Kyle. *Navigating Psychedelics: Trip Journal.* Psychedelics Today, 2021.
- Buller, Kyle. *Navigating Psychedelics: Integration Workbook.* Psychedelics Today, 2021
- Coder, Katherine E. *After the Ceremony Ends.* First Printing, 2017.
- Leary, Timothy. *The Psychedelic Experience.* Citadel Press, 1992.
- "Home." DoubleBlind Mag, 4 Apr. 2020, https://doubleblindmag.com/.

www.ingramcontent.com/pod-product-compliance
Lightning Source LLC
Chambersburg PA
CBHW072337300426
44109CB00042B/1655